Praise for *Conscience: The Duty to Obey and the Duty to Disobey*

"In *Conscience*, Rabbi Harold Schulweis displays a singular talent for weaving together a vast range of resources to speak of conscience and its demands. The result inspires an aesthetic appreciation of the intellectual depth and the human passions Rabbi Schulweis possesses. Much more importantly, Rabbi Schulweis employs these talents and this wisdom to provoke genuine moral concerns in his readers, and to convince them that their deeds can and must make a difference in the world."
—DR. DAVID ELLENSON, president, Hebrew Union College–Jewish Institute of Religion

"In this book, conscience is rightly presented as the basis of law and of life, as that internal moral sense by which we discern thoughtfully and responsibly when to obey and when to disobey."
—JUNE O'CONNOR, professor of Religious Studies, University of California, Riverside; past president, Society of Christian Ethics

"In this powerful and illuminating work, Rabbi Harold Schulweis, one of the most passionate voices of moral courage in our time, introduces us to the great Jewish tradition of dissent. The duty to disobey, Rabbi Schulweis insists, is as crucial to ethical life as the duty to obey. This work is sure to open eyes and hearts to the hidden call of conscience."
—RABBI NAOMI LEVY, author, *To Begin Again* and *Talking to God*

"In today's age caught between moral relativism and moral absolutes, this deeply spiritual and unabashedly human text emphasizes the importance of the call to individual conscience. It provides important guideposts for doing good when all around is moral collapse or blind conformity, and shines a light into the contemporary darkness and gives us all hope that we may find our way with courage and conviction."
—ABRAHAM H. FOXMAN, national director, Anti-Defamation League; author of *The Deadliest Lies: The Israel Lobby and the Myth of Jewish Control*

"Rabbi Harold Schulweis, a towering giant of conscience, has tirelessly redirected Jews and Christians to the core of God's concern—justice, compassion, selflessness, inclusion. In this extraordinary meditation, he blazes a pathway yet again, reminding us of the crucial role played by conscience in traditional and contemporary Jewish thought. Hooray for Harold Schulweis—the world is better because of him!"
—**RABBI BRADLEY SHAVIT ARTSON**, dean, Ziegler School of Rabbinic Studies and vice president, American Jewish University

"With this brilliant, inspiring and provocative synthesis of ancient texts, three millennia of philosophical wisdom and today's most urgent moral challenges, Rabbi Schulweis confirms his position as one of contemporary Jewry's most creative minds and powerful prophetic voices. His reconciliation of individual moral conscience with God's commandments and Judaism's legal tradition provides, at once, a distinctly Jewish and a bracing universal call to arms for a religiously authentic social justice activism."
—**RABBI DAVID DAVID SAPERSTEIN**, director, Religious Action Center of Reform Judaism

"Nothing less than a handbook for living in a time of terrorism and religious fundamentalism. How do religious believers discern what is immoral in their religion, and how can they find the strength of conscience and character to oppose those divine commandments, and those divine leaders, who are wrong? If you don't think the answer to this question matters, you aren't watching the news."
—**ROB ESHMAN**, editor-in-chief, *Jewish Journal of Greater Los Angeles*

"Engaging and clear style, this book documents the long Jewish concern for acting on conscience together with its critical importance for combating immoral laws, orders, and concepts of God and people. Teaches us how to cultivate a keen sense of conscience without abandoning social order. This is Judaism as it was meant to be understood and practiced."
—**RABBI ELLIOT N. DORFF**, author, *The Way Into Tikkun Olam* (Repairing the World)

"A most learned and intelligent discussion by one of the wisest spokesmen for the Jewish faith in the modern world. Rabbi Schulweis' analysis of the concept of conscience offers a most useful key to understanding how people can and do behave morally despite (rather than because of) their system of beliefs."
—NORBERT M. SAMUELSON, Harold and Jean Grossman Professor of Jewish Studies, Arizona State University

CONSCIENCE
The Duty to Obey and
the Duty to Disobey

Rabbi Harold M. Schulweis

JEWISH LIGHTS Publishing
Woodstock, Vermont

Conscience:
The Duty to Obey and the Duty to Disobey

2008 Hardcover Edition, First Printing
© 2008 by Harold M. Schulweis

Library of Congress Cataloging-in-Publication Data
Schulweis, Harold M.
Conscience : the duty to obey and the duty to disobey / Harold M. Schulweis.
p. cm.
Includes bibliographical references.
ISBN-13: 978-1-58023-375-0 (hardcover)
ISBN-10: 1-58023-375-9 (hardcover)
1. Conscience—Religious aspects—Judaism. 2. Obedience—Religious aspects—Judaism. 3. Prayer—Judaism. 4. Faith (Judaism) 5. Jewish ethics. I. Title.
BJ1286.C66S38 2008
296.3'6—dc22
2008034099

10 9 8 7 6 5 4 3 2 1

Manufactured in the United States of America
❀ Printed on recycled paper.
Jacket Design: Tim Holtz

Published by Jewish Lights Publishing
A Division of Longhill Partners, Inc.
Sunset Farm Offices, Route 4, P. O. Box 237
Woodstock, VT 05091
Tel: (802) 457-4000   Fax: (802) 457-4004
www.jewishlights.com

Dedicated to Rabbi Steven and Linda Jacobs
with profound friendship.

CONTENTS

ACKNOWLEDGMENTS

I am indebted to Stuart M. Matlins, publisher of Jewish Lights, for his patient and wise counsel; to Jane Jacobs, who typed and read the manuscript with punctuations of candor and concern; and Malkah, whose loving support remains indispensable.

INTRODUCTION

Two cautionary observations by two contemporary social critics haunt the subject of this study. Addressing the human condition in history, C. P. Snow writes, "When you think of the long and gloomy history of man, you will find more heinous crimes have been committed in the name of obedience than ever have been committed in the name of rebellion." History testifies to the damning terror brought upon civilization, in the name of obedience to authority. Conversely, the psychoanalyst Erich Fromm commented wryly that "human history began with an act of disobedience, and it is not unlikely that it will be terminated by an act of obedience." Fromm's reference to the Garden of Eden and the hell of genocide traces an ominous trajectory. The pervasive culture of total obedience to authority continues to cast its lugubrious shadow over a civilization in which 50 million human beings were systematically slaughtered by other human beings in the course of the twentieth century.

The admonitions of Snow and Fromm must be taken to heart. The good soldier, the loyal citizen, the devoted patriot, the compromising bureaucrat, and the true believer have led entire populations to succumb to the dying of conscience. The smothering culture of obedience fills the corridors of politics, industry, and the military. Unquestioning obedience to authority strangles the outbursts of moral protestation. Following the orders, decrees, and commandments of superiors is considered

1

sufficient justification for repression. And what of religion? Does it bear no responsibility for the rise and consequences of mindless conformity? Where is the outrage of the priests and of the parishioners of conscience heard today? Where is the spiritual preparation of the heart, teaching people when to intervene and how to brake the grinding wheels of conformity?

Religion often succumbs to the cult of "commandedness," too often assuming the role of the self-muted bystander to the callous and cruel insults to the human spirit. From the height of the pulpit, religion may sing the moral heroism of conscience, but closer to the congregation the encomium of conscience is transformed into stern admonitions of heresy, rebellion, and anarchy. Toward conscience, religion is ambivalent. Conscience remains forever suspect. In a world increasingly laden with unspeakable crimes against humanity all in the name of pious compliance, the lameness and lethal silence of the ecclesia are disillusioning. More is expected of religion. Does religion have the capacity, or more poignantly, does it have the will to counter the suppressive culture of obedience with the culture of moral courage and compassion? Can it motivate its disciples to shout "No!" in the presence of killers of the dream?

> Where is the spiritual preparation of the heart, teaching people when to intervene and how to brake the grinding wheels of conformity?

What follows in these pages is no brief for antinomianism—a society free of the discipline of law and the duty to obey. No society can endure without the duty to obey the collective wisdom of religion, which provides society with the continuity of inherited values in a time of indisputable chaos. What is disputable is the absolutism and inflexibility of the uncritical duty to obey. What to obey, whom to obey, where to obey, and when to obey are questions indispensable for a responsible and responsive faith. But without the courage to disobey, religion falls to bowing and kneeling postures. Religion is therefore obligated to make room for courageous moral dissent. It needs to provide sanctuary for those who will not be cowed by morally questionable decrees or edicts, else the religious duty to obey indiscriminately supports a totalitarian mind-set, and the world will continue to greet the genuflections of the piously compliant with cynical laughter.

Judaism and Conscience

How does my own faith fare before the assault on conscience and moribund moral sensibility? What does Judaism have to say to those who, on moral grounds, may challenge commander and commandment, rabbinic and scriptural narratives and laws? Was Baruch Spinoza accurate when he wrote, "The rule of right living, the worship and love of God, was to them [the Israelites] rather a bondage than true liberty, this gift and grace of the deity." Were Spinoza and those philosophers influenced by him (e.g., Kant, Hegel, and Fichte) correct in characterizing believing Jews as hopelessly duty-bound, "always to act under external activity and continually confess by these actions and thoughts that they were not their own masters, but were entirely under the control of others"?[1]

Such a presentation of Judaism is dishearteningly misleading because it is as commonly accepted by Jews as by non-Jews. One of the intentions of this book is to correct this understanding of Judaism as impersonal legislation and conforming obedience. Such characterization robs Judaism of its distinctive religious approach to law, ethics, and obligations.

Legislation and obedience are essential aspects of Judaism, but law and obedience in Judaism are controlled by a persistent moral conscience. No one is exempt from the critique of conscience—not patriarch, priest, prophet, rabbi, or even God—because conscience is embedded in the Jewish tradition. The laws and narratives of Judaism are not incorrigible within the tradition. Prescriptions and proscriptions, whatever their purported divine origin, are challenged, weighed, questioned, qualified, and even overturned with divine approval. In the Jewish tradition, human criticism is not stigmatized as heretical but honored by the One against whom the criticism is aimed.

Unqualified by conscience, law and obedience end in obdurate absolutism. The deep respect in Judaism for courage of conscience cultivates a sensibility significantly different from the conventional view of the religious believer who stands passive, acquiescent, and trembling before God and scripture. Conscience introduces an active, initiating religious temperament and a collegial relationship between the observant disciple and the author of the law. Contrary to those who split asunder the duty to obey and the duty to disobey, viewing them as contradictory, we Jews regard both duties as complementary. We must all strive to balance the duties to obey and to disobey so as to check the extremes of absolutism and the extremes of relativism, and to avoid falling into the arms of totalitarianism or anarchy.

> What to obey, whom to obey, where to obey, and when to obey are questions indispensable for a responsible and responsive faith.

Consider the metaphor I recall that best portrays the interdependence of the duty to obey and the duty to disobey: A window that is stuck open is as useless as one that is stuck closed. A window that is stuck open offers no protection from the gusty winds, while a window that is stuck closed isolates and suffocates. In either case, the flexibility of the sliding window is lost. Analogously, when the window of the duty to obey is stuck closed, it keeps out the fresh air that invigorates religious life and circulates relevance and responsiveness. When the window of the duty to disobey is stuck open, it leaves us unprotected from the relentless storms in our lives. Our windows are most useful when they slide between opened and closed, and discriminating conscience is the sliding window of a healthy religion.

A Word about Conscience

Conscience is a wisdom whose origin and practice are as puzzling as they are precious. As T. S. Eliot wrote, "Where is the wisdom we have lost in knowledge? Where is the knowledge we have lost in information?"[2] The word *conscience* is easier to illustrate than to define, and in fact the term has no translation in the classical Hebrew of the Bible or rabbinic tradition. Nevertheless, conscience is the subterranean wellspring beneath the stream of Jewish law, ethics, and theology. Modern Hebrew has coined an interesting word for conscience, *matzpun*, a term derived from the Hebrew *tzafun*, which connotes hiddenness. At the Passover seder, there is a concluding rite called *tzafun*, which in Hebrew means "hidden." It signals the search for the larger part of the previously broken matzah. The breaking of the matzah, the search for the hidden matzah, and the eating of that matzah at the end of the meal have no benedictions. They are all acts done in silence. Modern Hebrew has similarly coined the word *matzpen*, meaning compass, a term derived from the same root as hiddenness. Homiletically, conscience may be understood as the hidden inner compass that guides our lives and must be searched for and recovered repeatedly. At no time more

> Conscience is a wisdom whose origin and practice are as puzzling as they are precious.

than our own is this need to retrieve the shards of broken conscience more urgent.

I have turned to Judaism and its ancient traditional sources not because I believe that Judaism possesses an exclusive hold on conscience. I believe conscience is the lifeblood of all world religions. Nevertheless, the sources of Judaism are unique in placing a distinctive superordinate value on conscience as it relates to law, ethics, human nature, and the character of God.

The philosopher George Santayana noted that to speak in general without using any language in particular is, if not impossible, then foolhardy. I turn to Judaism because it is the particular language that I speak best. As I understand the particular Jewish understanding of conscience, it may be the most urgent contribution to world religion and civilization that Judaism can make.

1

CONSCIENCE
CONFRONTS GOD

I would rather be called a fool all my life than be called a godless man for one moment.

—AKABYA BEN MAHALALEL,
FIRST-CENTURY RABBINIC SCHOLAR

Some questions cut to the very core of faith. What is the appropriate response to divine laws that run against the grain of conscience? If biblical or rabbinic laws violate our personal moral sensibilities, are we left only with the alternative either to obey the revealed law or to shunt aside our mettlesome conscience? Must an avowedly immoral law, if claimed to be divinely given, be dutifully observed?

We have learned how to accommodate biblical cosmology and anthropology to Newton and Darwin, but the contradictions between law and conscience prove more troubling. The clash of divine law and morality confronts the believers' basic spiritual and moral rationale, the role ascribed to God as Sovereign Commander, and the degree of responsibility assigned to humanity. Is the human agent the servant or colleague of the divine authority? In this chapter, we will discuss the biblical precedent for humanity's interactions with God and our conflicts between divine law and human conscience.

7

Abraham and Moral Audacity

My earliest and lasting impression of the conflict between the word of God and the conscience of man began with Abraham's confrontation with God as depicted in the Bible.

The encounter between the father of the Jewish people and the God who has chosen him forecasts the role of moral conscience at the heart of the divine–human dialogue. That God would intend to visit judgment on the entire population of Sodom and Gomorrah is for Abraham grievously unfair:

> Abraham came forward and said, "Will You sweep away the innocent among the guilty? What if there should be fifty within the city; will You then wipe out the place, and not forgive it for the sake of the innocent fifty who are in it? Far be it from You to do such a thing, to bring death upon the innocent as well as the guilty, so that innocent and guilty fare alike. Far be it from You! Shall not the Judge of all the earth deal justly?" And the Lord answered, "If I find within the city of Sodom fifty innocent ones, I will forgive the whole place for their sake." (Gen. 18:23)

The overture to Abraham's robust altercation with God is introduced by God's self-revelation:

> Shall I hide from Abraham what I am about to do, since Abraham is to become a great and populous nation and all the nations of the earth are to bless themselves by him? For I have singled him out, that he may instruct his children and his posterity to keep the way of the Lord by doing what is just and right, in order that the Lord may bring about for Abraham what He has promised him. (Gen. 18:17)

God, who reveals his design to destroy the cities of sin, feels it necessary to explain this motivation so that Abraham may know how and why God functions in history. God's "justice and right-eousness" are the crucial moral predicates that inform the character of moral conscience in this story.

Once God reveals these moral traits, God is open to human moral critique. Without understanding God's justice and right-eousness, Abraham would have no alternative but to listen, heed, and quietly obey his Master's voice. With the self-revealing attributes of God, however, Abraham is empowered to measure God's design with the rod of God's own morality. God is not enmeshed in a veil of inscrutability, but is open to reciprocal exchange. The powerful bilateral dialogue that ensues is the matrix of multiple negotiations and altercations between a people and their God.

In the Abraham encounter, God is far from an implacable authoritarian commander designing plans that dare not be questioned. Abraham enters the throes of history as a divinely blessed moral hero. The event at Sodom introduces a paradigmatic model of behavior for a patriarch, prophet, and sage whose moral dissent against authority—human and divine—will not be dismissed as acts of treason against God. To the contrary, as we will see repeatedly in other divine–human conflicts, God not only accepts human moral criticism, but also is augmented by it. The theological implications and moral consequences of such a reciprocal dialogue affect Jewish belief, practice, and temperament.

> Spiritual audacity confronts authority with awe and respect. It appeals to an authority within authority, to conscience shared by divine believers and the Supreme Commander, and to the godliness within God.

We are conventionally raised to believe that Jewish faith demands unwavering obedience to the law and the law-giver. That attitude tends to cultivate a temperament of compliance and passivity. For conventional thinking, "talking back to God" smacks of heresy. But a significant genre of religious, moral, and spiritual audacity toward the divine authority—*chutzpah klapei shmaya*—finds a place of honor in Jewish religious thought.

By "spiritual audacity" I do not mean what is commonly referred to as chutzpah. Spiritual audacity against God is not belief mocked. Chutzpah is usually associated with contrariness, the kind of nerve told of the young man who, having murdered his parents, pleads for clemency on the grounds that he is an orphan. Spiritual audacity, by contrast, confronts authority with awe and respect. It appeals to an authority within authority, to conscience shared by divine believers and the Supreme Commander, and to the godliness within God.

Moses Nullifies God's Law

God's "justice and righteousness" are no more hidden from Moses than they were concealed from Abraham. One striking rabbinic legend imagines Moses's displeasure with an important segment in the second commandment. For Moses, that God should visit "the iniquity of the fathers upon the children to the third and fourth generation" (Exod. 20:5) is an unacceptable form of group punishment akin to the morally indiscriminate punishment of Sodom. Challenging God's pronouncement of the punishment of the sons for the sins of the fathers, Moses argues with God, against God, and in the name of God. Moses engages God with fierce moral logic:

> Sovereign of the Universe, consider the righteous-
> ness of Abraham and the idol worship of his father
> Terach. Does it make moral sense to punish the
> child for the transgressions of the father? Sovereign
> of the Universe, consider the righteous deeds of
> King Hezekiah, who sprang from the loins of his evil
> father King Achaz. Does Hezekiah deserve Achaz's

punishment? Consider the nobility of King Josiah, whose father Amnon was wicked. Should Josiah inherit the punishment of Amnon? (Num. Rabbah, Hukkat XIX, 33)

Trained to view God as an unyielding authoritarian proclaiming immutable commands, we might expect that Moses will be severely chastised for his defiance. Who is this finite, errant, fallible, human creature to question the explicit command of the author of the Ten Commandments? The divine response to Moses, according to the rabbinic moral imagination, is arresting:

> By your life Moses, you have instructed Me. Therefore I will nullify My words and confirm yours. Thus it is said, "The fathers shall not be put to death for the children, neither shall the children be put to death for the fathers." (Deut. 24:16)

Far from being chastised by God, Moses is rewarded by having his own human critique recorded later in the sacred text in Moses's own name. "As it is written in the book of the Law of Moses, as the Lord commanded, saying 'The father shall not be put to death'" (Num. Rabbah 19:33). The God of the sages does not merely ordain; God also listens. Even after God passes judgment, God allows humans who have been endowed with the moral competence and courage to challenge the Sovereign Deity—to instruct.

God's openness to human critique is reiterated throughout the rabbinic stories of disputations between God and Jewish religious heroes. For example, in protest against God's threatening imprecations toward those who worshipped the golden calf, Moses argues against God's punitive intent: "Sovereign of the Universe, how can Israel realize what they have done, seeing that they have been raised in Egypt?" Moses reminds God that the Ten Commandments were not given to the Children of

Israel, but to Moses himself, and that therefore the Children of Israel should not stand in violation of the law. It is Moses alone who may be judged culpable. Hearing the argument, God concedes, "By your life, Moses, you have spoken well" (Exod. Rabbah, Ki Tissa 47:9).

In yet another biblical episode, elaborated by the rabbinic commentary, Moses defies God's command to make war with Sihon, a people who have not interfered with Israel (Deut. 2:34). Moses is explicitly commanded by the Supreme Commander to make war, but he disobeys the divine order and instead sends messengers to proclaim peace to Sihon. God's enthusiastic approving response to Moses's violation of the command declares, "By your life Moses, I shall cancel my own words and proclaim yours." The lesson: people of faith may intercede and divine imperatives are subject to correction.

Rabbinic midrashim of dissent are numerous and religiously significant. These midrashim, or rabbinic parables, are elaborate metaphors and legends that fill the moral lacunae of biblical narratives, unburdening the believer from a submissive reading of scriptures and a subservient stance toward the Sovereign Commander. In midrash, God hears moral arguments and cancels decrees. In this way, the biblical text is not the last but the first word of God. The Bible is not a closed book, but open to the multiple interpretation of its sages. Embedded in the sharp divine–human exchange is the presence and power of conscience to refine the law.

Moses Cites Scripture to God

God is not alone. God needs the human being. The human being is God's closest and indispensable ally. The divine and the human are morally co-related. God intervenes on behalf of humanity, and humanity intervenes on behalf of God. In a compelling midrash based on a biblical narrative, God is furious at the people of Israel for worshipping the golden calf at the foot

of Mount Sinai. Angered, God exclaims, "Now let Me alone, that
My wrath may wax hot against them" (Exod. 32:9). In the interpretation of the Talmud (Berachoth 32a) and midrash (Exod.
Rabbah 43:3–4) Moses hears God's odd expression "Let Me
alone" as a cue for Moses's
active intervention. Who is
there to restrain God but the
human listener? Moses's action
toward God is analogous to a
man seizing the garment of his
fellow and declaring, "I will not
let you go until you forgive and
pardon me." In the same way,
Moses prayed before the Holy

> The Bible is not a closed
> book. Embedded in the
> sharp divine–human
> exchange is the presence
> and power of conscience
> to refine the law.

One to save his people, "until a fire seized him" (Exod. Rabbah,
Ki Tissa 42:9, and B. Berachoth 32a). The confrontation is rem-
iniscent of Abraham's critique of God's intention at Sodom and
Gomorrah. Here Moses pleads that it would be a profanity for
God to attack Israel.

The ideal prophet, sages declare, "defends Israel before
God and God before Israel" (*Mekilta de Rabbi Ishmael, Pischa 1*).
The ideal prophet is Jeremiah, who defends the "son" (Israel)
before the "father" (God), and defends the "father" before the
"son." For Moses, conscience is the intermediary between God
and Israel. Throughout his career, Moses places himself in the
middle, defending both the dignity of God and the dignity of
God's people. Moses is no sycophantic follower. Moses admon-
ished God because of Israel and reproached Israel because of
God. To Israel, Moses said, "You have sinned a great sin," and to
God he said, "Lord, why does Your wrath wax hot against Your
people?"

Throughout much of the rabbinic midrashic tradition, we
meet the dignity of the believer who stands toe-to-toe with God.
In one midrashic exchange, Moses addresses God as a virtual
equal. God and Moses have been at each other, God arguing

that Israel has betrayed the law, and Moses pleading with God in
defense of Israel's innocence. The scale of justice lies evenly balanced. Moses approaches God, declaring, "You God say You will
smite them, and I say pardon them." He concludes, "The matter
is evenly balanced; we will see who will prevail: You, Lord, or I."
Rabbi Berekya adds that God then said to Moses: "By your life,
Moses, you have nullified My will and yours prevails" (Num.
Rabbah 16:25 and Deut. Rabbah 5:13).

Throughout these rabbinic stories, we face a unique Jewish
religious anthropology. The human being is no robotic instrument of God's play, but rather a person endowed with a dignity
that encourages him or her to oppose the master, to defend the
accused, and often to prevail. The human challenge receives
due honor from the allegedly vanquished Deity. Such legends,
canonized in the midrashic literature, break the image of the
believer as a slave to the master, or the critic dismissed as a rebel
without a true cause.

Moses Frees God

In a stunning midrashic reading of a biblical text, Moses
astoundingly frees God from God's own vow (Exod. Rabbah
43:4). In the episode of the golden calf, God struggles with a
self-made dilemma. On the one hand, God has taken an oath to
destroy the Children of Israel because of their worship of the
golden calf; on the other hand, God is persuaded by Moses to
override that oath. But how can God violate the oath inasmuch
as God is bound by the dictates of God's own words? God
declares, "I cannot retract an oath which has proceeded from
My mouth." Moses then appeals to God's own laws: "Did You,
God, not give me the power of annulment of oaths by saying,
'When a man vows a vow to the Lord, or swears an oath to bind
his soul, he himself cannot break his word' (Num. 30:3), yet a
scholar may absolve his vows if he consults him?" "Come to me."
Then Moses says, "It is only right that You should annul Your

own oath. You should be the first to follow Your annulment through me." God accedes to Moses's argument. Moses wraps himself in his cloak in the manner of a sage while God stands before him asking for the annulment of the divine vow. Moses asks God, "Do you regret now Your vow?" and God replies, "I regret now the evil which I said I would do to my .people." Hearing God's response, Moses rules: "Be it absolved for You. There is neither vow nor oath any longer" (Exod. Rabbah 43:4). God has been liberated by Moses's use of God's law.

Throughout such rabbinic homilies, the elevation of the religious hero is indicative of a reciprocal divine–human relationship radically different from that of master and slave. God's dependence on humans is no denigration of God's authority but rather an elevation of God's recognition of human collegiality.

God and humankind are interdependent. The Bible informs us that when the Children of Israel sinned against God, God was offended and left the tent of Israel in anger. In sympathy with God, Moses, too, left the tent of Israel in anger. According to a rabbinic reading, Moses is rebuked by God. The Lord spoke to Moses face-to-face: "Have I not made a condition with you that when you are angry I appease you, and when I am angry, you will appease Me? Turn back, Moses, and return to the camp" (Exod. Rabbah 45:2). Here, the complementary role of God and the religious disciple is poignantly expressed. God declares, "Shall two angry faces put hot water into the drink? Have I not told you that when I am in anger, you are to placate Me, and when you are in anger, I will placate you?" (Exod. Rabbah 45:2).

A related midrash demonstrates the loving interdependence of God and the religious hero. When Moses is about to die, God asks:

> Who now will stand against Me on the day of wrath?
> Who shall protect Israel in the house of My anger?

> Who will stand up for My children in the great end
> of days, and who will speak up for them when they
> sin? (Midrash Tanhuma, Buber, ed.)

Prophetic moral conscience does not exempt the claims of
the prophet, not even the prophet of prophets, Moses himself. The prophet whose prophesies are spoken in God's name
is not invulnerable to moral critique. Moreover, the prophet's
foretelling and predications may be overturned.

The intertwined relationship between the divine and the
human is proudly announced by the psalmist: "He, God, would
have destroyed them had not Moses, His chosen one, confronted Him in the breach to avert His wrath" (Ps. 106:23).

Four Dissenting Prophets

Prophetic conscience is not intimidated by the status of the
prophet. The predictions and judgments of the prophet who
claims to speak in the name of God may be questioned and
contradicted, his prophesies overturned. No prophetic figure
is more respected than Moses, who spoke to God "face-to-face."
Yet the sages in the Talmud relate that other prophets revoked
some of the very prophesies that Moses proclaimed in God's
name (Makkoth 24a). Moses prophesied four adverse sentences upon Israel, but four prophets revoked them all. Moses
had said, "And Israel shall dwell in safety alone, at the fountain
of Jacob" (Deut. 33:28). In other words, Israel is safe in isola-
tion, but not safe among the nations. Amos the prophet
demurred and revoked that prophesy, appealing to God.
"Then said I, O Lord God, cease, I beseech You; how shall
Jacob stand alone? For he is small." The verse goes on, "The
Lord repented concerning this; 'This also shall not be,' saith
the Lord" (Amos 7:2–6).

Moses had also passed verdict on Israel, saying, "And
among the nations you will have no repose" (Deut. 28:65). The

prophet Jeremiah opposed Moses's prophesy: "Thus says the Lord: 'The people that were left of the sword have found grace in the wilderness, even Israel. When I go to affirm him, I go to afford him rest'" (B. Makkoth 24a).

Regarding God's visiting the iniquity of the fathers upon the children, the prophet Ezekiel contradicted the biblical verse spoken by Moses, declaring, "The soul that sinneth, it shall die" (Ezek. 18:3–4).

When Moses prophesied in God's name, "And you shall perish among the nations" (Lev. 26:38), the prophet Isaiah countered and contradicted Moses's biblical statement: "And it shall come to pass in that day that a great horn shall be blown (and they shall come that were lost in the land of Assyria)" (Isa. 27:13).

The four prophets are incensed at the judgments proclaimed by Moses in God's name, and they contradict the law of Moses in order to arrogate the claim of critical conscience. Not even the greatest of prophets, they imply, may claim to speak the final word.

Hannah Hurls Words Toward Heaven

God and human beings are not bound by unyielding fate, as we learn from the biblical Hannah (1 Sam. 10), a woman of sorrowful spirit. Hannah bemoans her barrenness and prays for a child. Her petitions go unanswered and her womb is closed. Hannah appeals to God's mercy:

> Sovereign of the Universe, among all the things You have created in a woman, You have not created one without a purpose—eyes to see, ears to hear, a nose to smell, a mouth to speak, hands to do work, legs to walk with, breasts to suckle. These breasts you have put on my heart, are they not to suckle? (B. Berachoth 31b)

Hannah will not be stymied by her unanswered petition. She presents God with a plaintive parable:

> The King made feasts for his servants, and a poor man came and stood by the door and cried out, "Give me a bite." No one paid attention, so he forced his way into the presence of the King and said, "Your Majesty, out of all the feasts which you have made, is it so hard in your eyes to give me one bite?"

Her plea for a child remains unanswered, but Hannah will not take no for an answer. Hannah turns God's law to her favor by devising a plan consistent with the biblical law. With deliberacy, she shuts herself up with another man in the full knowledge of her husband, Elkanah, knowing that she will be cleared of any accusations. The biblical law states unequivocally that if "her husband grows jealous of the feigned intimacy, he is to test his wife by taking her to the elders who will compel her to drink the bitter waters of those who are suspected of infidelity by their husbands." The biblical law states that if the woman is innocent, she will be cleared and will conceive a child. Hannah spoke "insolently against heaven," and Hannah prevailed. She bore a child she named Samuel, meaning "I asked the Lord for him."

> Moral conscience will not allow evil to be called good, and it will not allow easy rationalization of tragic events to justify God's disengagement from the world.

Hannah's plaintive defiance led Got to move from the throne of justice to the throne of mercy. Elsewhere, the sages opine that God prays for such exchanges. In the Talmud, God prays, "May it be My will that My mercy prevail over My other attributes so that I may deal with My children in the attainment of mercy, and on their behalf stop short of the limit of strict justice" (B. Berachoth 7a). The petitionary prayers of Hannah result in God's self-petitioning prayer to elevate mercy within the law of strict justice.

The Psalmist Awakes the Slumbering

In the midst of ecstatic praise of God, reality breaks in on the psalmist. In the presence of evil, praise of God seems blasphemous. The integrity of conscience does not allow for sycophantic piety.

Moral conscience will not allow evil to be called good, and it will not allow easy rationalization of tragic events to justify God's disengagement from the world. It is not a question of belief in God's existence but a challenge to God as bystander who gazes idly at the shed blood of innocence and does not intervene. The psalmist's conscience will not accept the excuses of the human or divine bystander.

The Talmud (Sotah 48a) recounts that in the time of the Second Temple, the Levites stood upon the dais as "awakeners of the Lord" and would read out loud the forty-fourth chapter of the Book of Psalms. The psalm is both reverent and accusatory, praising and criticizing God: "You let them devour us like sheep, disbursed us among the nations." The psalmist anticipates the type of defense that conventionally blames Israel for its own slaughter and humiliation, and will not compromise his moral indignation over God's neutrality.

> All this has come upon us, yet we have not forgotten You, or been false to Your covenant. We have not forgotten the name of our God and we will not accept blame for our lot. It is for Your sake that we are slain all day long, that we are regarded as sheep to be slaughtered.

The contentious psalmist would shake God from somnolence:

> Rouse Yourself. Why do You sleep, O Lord? Awaken,
> do not reject us forever. Why do You hide Your face,
> ignoring our affliction and distress? We lie prostrate
> in the dust; our body clings to the ground. Arise
> and help us, redeem us as befits Your faithfulness.

Natural Moral Sensibility

The passages from the Bible and Talmud and the midrashim we
have examined are but a small number in the genre of Jewish
religious dissent. The meaning of their assertiveness deserves
thoughtful consideration. God's image as a celestial despot
whose verdicts dare not be contradicted is transformed, and the
moral responsibilities assigned to the human partner of the
covenant are markedly increased.

The genre of spiritual chutzpah in the rabbinic tradition
entails a deep Jewish conviction in the moral power and piety of
conscience. Regrettably, the appreciation of heroic piety is
rarely transmitted to the contemporary Jewish student or parish-
ioner. The first chief rabbi of Palestine, Abraham Isaac Kook,
called attention to the interdependence of "natural, moral sensibility" and "religious observance." In his *Oroth Ha Kodesh*[1]
(Section 4e) he wrote:

> It is forbidden for religious behavior to compromise
> a personal, natural, moral sensibility. If it does, our
> fear of heaven is no longer pure. An indication of
> its purity is that our nature and moral sense
> becomes more exalted as a consequence of reli-
> gious inspiration. But if these opposites occur, then
> the moral character of the individual or group is
> dismissed by religious observance, and we have cer-
> tainly been mistaken in our faith.

In Judaism, belief in God and religious observance do not override conscienceless behavior. Where conscience finds moral fault in purportedly divine imperatives, the imperatives need to be reexamined. Abraham Joshua Heschel wrote of the transcendent God as "He to whom our conscience is open."[2] I would add that conscience lies between God and the human being and is the nexus that binds God and Israel in reciprocal covenant.

2

HUMAN CONSCIENCE AND DIVINE LEGISLATION

Real human progress depends not so much on inventive ingenuity as on conscience.

—ALBERT EINSTEIN

Could the Rabbis of tradition possibly question the morality of a law ascribed to God? And if not, what should be done with those divine commands that violate our moral conscience?

"A Divine Command cannot be branded as immoral … morality (our sense of morality) recedes before a Divine command."[1] Such is the conclusion arrived at by the eminent Talmudic scholar Rabbi David Weiss-Halivni. From the viewpoint of the sages of the Talmud, Rabbi Weiss-Halivni argues, whatever is written in the Torah cannot be declared immoral. If morally troubling religious laws were seemingly evident, the sages might rectify them through legal interpretations, but certainly not by oral refutation. Rabbinic interpretations, Weiss-Halivni continues, "usually follow exegetical consistencies rather than moral dilemmas." Rabbinic juridical skills, not arguments from conscience, may extricate us from avowedly unjust laws. Moral conscience did not, may not, and cannot stand on the same dais as law.

The distinguished philosopher and talmudist Yeshayahu Leibowitz assumes a similar, if sterner, stance: "The Torah and the prophets never appeal to moral conscience, for such an appeal is always suspect as a possible expression of idolatry." For Leibowitz, "Conscience is not to be found in the Hebrew Bible." Guidance of the morality of Torah law is "an atheistic, indeed an idolatrous concept." Halacha, religious law, does not "tolerate the concept of ethics."[2] Ethics is, at best, suspect; at worse, subversive.

Another contemporary Orthodox philosopher, Michael Wyschograd, asserts that "conscience does not even figure in either Jewish theology or in history."[3] I argue, to the contrary, that moral conscience played, plays, and must continue to play a role in halacha. Ignoring halachic conscience only serves to *de*-moralize Jewish law. Indeed, the sages explained that the destruction of the Second Temple took place despite widespread pious study and dutiful practice of the Torah (B. Yoma 9b). More than law is revealed in Torah. More than obedience to the law is demanded of a believing Jew. Moral conscience ought not be treated as an extra-legal moral faculty floating above biblical and rabbinic law. Halachic conscience functions internally within the law and has successfully altered and even abrogated laws that are morally offensive. It is important, therefore, to uncover within the limits of the law the depth of moral conscience inherent in the halachic process.

There are a number of rabbinic interpretations of biblical law that demonstrate the crucial role conscience plays in confronting some of the morally contentious laws in the Bible. The following illustrations confirm my conviction that so-called disobedient rabbinic decisions are far from esoteric, eccentric, or inconsequential for the halachic mind. In fact, they seriously inform the Jewish understanding of divine and human nature and the distinctive character of their interrelationship in the covenant.

Rabbinic legal practice presupposes the corrigibility of the divine text and the authority of that text. Judging from these bold midrashic interpretations, it is apparent that the Torah is not the final word of God to the sage. God is appealed to beyond the boundaries of law and is not bound by that very own fiat. God can be moved. God's mind, heart, and words can be changed. God can announce a verdict and thereafter revoke it.

This is one of the lessons derived from the prophet Jonah, who discovered that the God he sought to escape could be moved by the repentance of the citizens of Nineveh. Because they repented, God repented of the implied punishment. Jonah learned that the changing heart of God is not a sign of vacillation but a tribute to God's compassionate generosity. Jonah's mind initially saw God as an implacable sovereign authority and even argued with God that the implied punishment be carried out. But he came to learn that the Sovereign of the Universe is not an inflexible master, nor are God's disciples subjugated servants. "And God saw what they did, how they were turning back from their evil ways, and God renounced the punishment He had planned to bring upon them and not carry it out" (Jon. 3:10). The Torah can be both appealed and repealed.

> Halacha must have conscience. The law and the morality of Torah are of one piece.

If God's decree, directly given, is subject to being challenged on moral grounds, so too can God's laws (halacha). Within the following midrashim we find human beings endowed with moral competence and the courage to challenge and correct divine judgments. We discover a believer who is active, initiating, energetic, and unafraid. Most important, we discover God's enthusiastic approval of human critique and the exercise of the logic of moral conscience.

Halacha must have conscience. In the Talmud, Rabbi Yochanan opines that Jerusalem was destroyed because the Rabbis ruled solely in passive accommodation with biblical law: "They based their judgments strictly upon biblical law, and did not go beyond the requirements of the law" (Baba Metzia 30b).

Although such a statement is far from contradicting biblical law, it warns that the letter of the biblical law must not be allowed to crush the spirit of halachic conscience. The law and the morality of Torah are of one piece.

Were people aware of the Jewish legal conscience in the tradition, they would deal with certain objectionable laws without defensiveness, evasion, or embarrassment. They would recognize that throughout Jewish life, changing social conditions called for different applications of the law.

Rabbinic Legal Conscience

In a celebrated Talmudic passage (Baba Metzia 83a), the porters of Rabbah bar Hana broke a barrel of his wine. Rabbah seized the clothing of the porters, citing the law that a worker is legally responsible for any loss caused through his own negligence. The porters then appealed to Rav, who ruled that Rabbah must give them back their clothes. Rabbah asks, "*Dina hachi?*" "Is this the law?" Rav replies, "Even so." Rav justifies his halachic ruling by citing the biblical verse from Proverbs 2:20: "That you may walk in the ways of good men." Rabbah accepts Rav's ruling and returns the garments to the porters. The porters come again to Rav, this time arguing that they have toiled all day long and are hungry. "Are we to get nothing?" Rav again orders Rabbah to give the workers their wages. Rabbah once more questions Rav's judgment—"*Dina hachi?*" Rav answers, "Even so," and cites the conclusion of Proverbs 2:20, "And you shall keep the path of righteousness."

Rabbah wonders at Rav's ruling. After all, the biblical text in Exodus 2:3 declares that "we are not to favor the cause of the poor because he is poor." Moreover, the sage Rabbi Akiba stated that in matters of objective law, "no compassion is to be shown" (Midrash, Ketuboth 9:2). But Rav's biblical justification for his halachic ruling is clearly based on Jewish moral principles. We are "to keep the paths of the righteous" because "our ways are ways of pleasantness" (Prov. 3:17). Rav's choice of scriptural citations echoes the biblical verse in Exodus 22:25, which teaches:

> If you lend money to the poor and take his hire and take his garment as a pledge you shall restore it to him before the sun sets; for it is his only clothing, the garment of his skin, wherein shall he sleep? And it shall come to pass when he cries out to Me that I will heed, for I am compassionate.

What assumptions underlie the exchange between Rabbah and Rav? For Rav, compassionate conscience is embedded in the law. Moral conscience is not an extraneous virtue outside the province of the law itself. Law and morals are complementary aspects of the halachic process. Without an inclusive understanding of the interdependence of law and morality, conscience is estranged from the halachic process and is deemed adversarial toward the law. Rav's ruling evidences the role of halachic conscience. "Even so. This is the law." Conscience is integral to the practice of the law.

Laws That Never Were and Never Will Be

My grandfather came to the synagogue because he was Jewish. His grandchildren come to the synagogue to become Jewish. Therein lies the deepest challenge to the contemporary synagogue. Seated in the synagogue, the grandchildren listen dutifully to the Bible chanted, look at the English translation, and, at times, whisper their disappointment with those biblical passages they find morally incomprehensible.

How should contemporary Jews be taught to deal with morally flawed edicts? Are they to stifle their moral sense or throw aside the biblical law? Most are raised to believe that inasmuch as the Bible is divinely revealed, its laws are beyond criticism. Fear of violating Torah leaves them feeling guilty for their disbelief, or perhaps secretly proud of their moral superiority to the arcane Torah text. The moral failure of the text before them is unsettling and the sanctity of scriptures appears debased. If only these Jews knew that they had distinguished rabbinic ancestors who, sensing the jarring ethics of certain laws, did something creative to supersede them.

What did the Rabbis do when they considered a biblical or rabbinic mandate to be palpably unfair? Although they did not and would not excise the biblical law, they ingeniously interpreted the troubling injunction out of existence.

One rabbinic strategy for dealing with a morally disturbing law was to render it de facto inapplicable. The legal methods used by the Rabbis to achieve such legal maneuvers may appear convoluted, strained, or forced, but they are based on moral motivation. Rabbinic strategies were used as legal means for moral ends, and the laws chosen to be circumvented or abrogated were precisely those that rubbed against the grain of rabbinic conscience.

Modernity owns no exclusive claim on morality. Our discontent with certain narratives and biblical mandates are not confined to modern sensibilities. The sages of antiquity felt that discontent just as deeply.

The Rebellious Son

The Torah includes a harsh passage that deals with the stubborn and rebellious son. The biblical law calls for parents to lay hold of their wayward and defiant son who will not heed them, and bring him before the elders of the city (Deut. 22:18–21). Should the gluttonous and drunken son be found guilty, he is to be stoned. "So shall you do away with the evil from the midst of you; and all Israel shall hear and fear." The Rabbis of the Talmud were disturbed by the severity of this law. In response, they piled up so many legal conditions that the biblical law became de facto unenforceable. The sages ruled that the stubborn and rebellious son referred to in the Bible cannot be a minor child;

that both parents must be united in their complaint; that both parents must resemble each other in voice and height; that for a first offense, a son had to be formally warned and flogged by the local court of three; that if the son continued in his obdurate behavior, he was to be tried by a court of twenty-three; but that he can be executed only when the first three judges were present. "The wayward and defiant son" may be subject to the penalty described in the Torah only from the time that he produces two hairs and until he grows a beard (by which is meant his pubic hair, not facial hair). As a minor, the wayward son is exempt from punishment, since a minor does not come within the scope of the commandments. Moreover, because the Bible uses the word "son," only a son, and not a daughter, is subject to this law.

In the end, the Rabbis agreed that the biblical law of the wayward and defiant son "has never been and never will be." Such a bold declaration annulled a biblical law from past, present, or future implementation. The Rabbis themselves wondered, "If the law never had been and never will be, why was this biblical law written at all?" They answered, "So that you may study it and receive reward for its study." In this way, the disturbing law was treated as an academic exercise, a topic of theoretical interest but without practical consequences. Rabbi Simon, supporting the nullification of this biblical law, appealed to the moral conscience of his colleagues, "Because one eats a tartmar of meat and drinks a log of Italian wine, shall his father and mother have him stoned?" (B. Sanhedrin 71a).

Those not knowing the moral ground of the rabbinic nullification of the biblical law rightly find the severe Bible passage upsetting. But to read the Bible as the last word, stripped of the moral commentary and interpretations of the rabbinic tradition, is to rob the tradition of the evolving moral dynamics within the halachic process. The congregation has not heard about the religious duty to disobey bad laws in the name of Jewish moral conscience. They must be shown that the sources of Jewish conscience are not novel, modern, or extrinsic but rooted in ancient halachic tradition.

Idolatrous Cities, Leprous Houses

In accordance with biblical law (Deut. 13:13–19), a city tainted with idolatry is to be destroyed. The Rabbis again concluded that this biblical law "never has been and never will be" (B. Sanhedrin 71a). Is it conceivable that a city should have no innocent citizen? Echoing Abraham's arguments with God concerning the destruction of Sodom, the Talmudic sages qualified this biblical law out of existence. The deleterious consequences led them to render the law of the apostate city inoperative.

In a similar manner and for similar reasons, the biblically ordained destruction of a leper's house (Lev. 14:34) was proclaimed by the Rabbis to be a verdict that "never has been and never will be" (Lev. 71a). Again, the sages turned practice into theory, an ingenious technique to abolish a law considered immoral without erasing the text. While the triumph of conscience over the command is accomplished by legalistic methods, the implicit rationale that promoted such juridical dexterity is clearly moral. If a putative divine law appears immoral, Jewish tradition is empowered to rectify it.

Capital Punishment

The Rabbis made no secret of their aversion to biblical laws that mandated capital punishment. Yet they could not deny that for a variety of crimes, capital punishment was biblically mandated. The sages, vexed by the practice of capital punishment, threw a mounting series of legal roadblocks before the execution of capital punishment. Death sentences were virtually impossible to impose. In matters of capital punishment for murder, the Rabbis did not admit circumstantial evidence. The intent of the wrongdoer had to be carefully examined, and the potential criminal had to be forewarned (*hatra'ah*) by two sworn witnesses. The Rabbis insisted that the suspect must know the full consequences of his premeditated crime and understand the exact punishment for his contemplated design:

> They [the court] said to him: "Refrain, do not commit that act for it is a transgression and you have become liable to the death penalty or to lashes." If the wrongdoer remains silent (not seeming to understand or acknowledge the forewarning) he cannot be sentenced as guilty. Only if the one warned of the full consequences of the deed declares, "I know it, and in spite of that I will do the act," was he considered to be worthy of execution.[4]

The forewarning was to be made immediately before the act, and should the act be delayed, a new forewarning was required.

In the Mishnah (Makkoth 1:10) we read that "A Sanhedrin which executes one person in seven years is called a destructive court." Rabbi Eleazar ben Azariah contends that even "one execution in seventy years" would justify calling a Sanhedrin a "destructive court." Rabbi Tarphon and Rabbi Akiba further declare, "Were we members of the court, no man would ever be executed." Again, the underlying moral sensibility of the Talmudic Rabbis turned de jure legislation into de facto abrogation. Jewish law is exalted not as an exhibition of legal ingenuity as much as for its moral implications.

Sotah: The Ordeal of Jealousy

By what sort of logic are divine laws overturned? Consider the Rabbis faced with the morally offensive, biblically prescribed laws of Sotah, the test for a wife suspected of adultery. Brought before the sanctuary, the suspected wife was to drink a holy potion, the water of bitterness, and to hear the priest pronounce a fearful curse. Should she be guilty, the water will make her body swell and her thigh fall away. To this curse the woman was to respond, "Amen, amen" (Num. 5:12–31). The Rabbis were so incensed and repulsed by the law that he abolished it with the following argument: "If you husbands are above reproach, the water will put your wife to the proof. But if not, it will not put your wives to the proof." The biblical ordeal of jealousy was put to an end by the moral logic of conscience. Rabbi Yochanan ben Zakkai rose to further oppose the hypocrisy of the accusing husbands, citing the prophet Hosea:

> I will not punish your daughters when they commit whoredom, nor your daughters-in-law when they themselves commit adultery, for they themselves turn aside with harlots and sacrifice with prostitution; and a people that does not understand shall be trodden down. (Hosea 4:14)

This verse from Hosea was chosen because the gender bias in the laws of Sotah was felt to be evidently egregious. The biblical law was annulled (M. Sotah 9:9).

Illegitimacy: When Conscience Fails

Conscience is not always victorious, yet even in defeat its irrepressible voice resonates. According to Jewish law, for instance, a Jewish child who is the offspring of a forbidden union (e.g., a child born out of adulterous or incestuous relations, or from parents who had remarried without securing a religious divorce) is legally prohibited from marrying into his or her people (Deut. 23:3). Some explain the pariah status ascribed to the child as the way the tradition sought to deter illicit relationships, but the sages were uneasy with the ruling. The midrash singles out Daniel the Tailor, who is outraged by the law: "If the father of the child had illicit sexual relations, how did the child sin?" Daniel accuses the rabbinic Sanhedrin that so rules as callous.

"Who is there to comfort the children?" Daniel accuses the Sanhedrin for sustaining a law that causes innocent children to cry. The sages acknowledge the justice of Daniel's indignation, but in this instance they feel bound to the biblical law that overrides human moral sense. Nevertheless, Daniel's protest moves the conscience of the Rabbis to declare that "The bastards will enter the world to come, for God will comfort them and in the days of the Messiah illegitimate bastards will be considered pure" (Eccles. Rabbah 4:1).

> Conscience is not always victorious, yet even in defeat its irrepressible voice resonates.

Conscience, even when muffled, leaves its indelible imprint. Daniel challenges the rabbis today, as he did the Rabbis of his time, to legitimize the blameless and not wait passively for Messianic intervention.

The Chained Woman

When innocent lives are ruined by laws, conscience calls for more than acquiescence. To change a bad law calls for compassionate conscience and moral courage. Along with the treatment of the status of illegitimacy, the tragic role of chained women (*agunah*) also cries out for the exercise of halachic conscience today.

In the rabbinic tradition, a woman whose marriage was de facto terminated (e.g., her husband is missing in war or has for whatever reason abandoned her) cannot remarry without a legal Jewish divorce (*get*). But since husbands alone in the tradition have the right to initiate a divorce, the abandoned woman is "chained" and cannot marry another. Halachically she still remains married to her missing or recalcitrant husband. The chained woman may be free to remarry only if there are witnesses to the death of her husband.

But who is qualified to be a witness? The Bible (Deut. 19:15) explicitly declares, "At the mouth of two witnesses or at

the mouth of three witnesses shall a matter be established."
How, in the absence of witnesses, can the manacles of the *agu-nah* be loosened? Despite biblical stipulations, Rabbi Gamliel
the Elder courageously married the chained widows of such
men on the basis of testimony offered by one witness alone, or
even if a witness were a woman, slave, bondwoman, relative non-Jew, or apostate Jew—persons who would not under scriptural
law be accepted as legitimate witnesses. Rabbi Gamliel followed
the path of compassionate conscience (Midrash, Yevamoth 16:7).
Tragically, even today the *agunah* remains enchained in certain
rabbinic circles. Injustice violates the dignity of the *agunah* and
awaits, in certain law-abiding circles, moral reparation.

Maimonides: Within the Letter of the Law

Conscience without law is capricious. Law without conscience is
heartless. How can law and conscience coexist?

In a moving ruling from the twelfth century, codifier of
Jewish law Moses Maimonides ruled that halachically, "it is per-mitted to work a heathen slave with vigor, i.e., with the same
kind of harsh treatment with which the Egyptian's taskmaster
imposed upon the Hebrew slave." Although Maimonides could
not deny biblical law, he would not let that law stand as the
definitive last Jewish word. Halachic conscience compelled
Maimonides to add, "Though this is law, the quality of piety and
wisdom calls for a person to be merciful and preserve justice and
not make his yoke heavy upon the slave or distress him; but give
him eat and drink of all foods and drink."[5] The great Jewish
legalist understood that moral piety and wisdom must both be
part of the law.

To sustain his advocacy to act beyond the letter of the law,
Maimonides cites Job's declaration of Jewish universalism: "If I
did despise the cause of my manservant and maidservant, when
they contended with me, then I would be guilty. Did not He, that
made me in the womb, make him and did not One fashion us in

the womb?" (Job 31:13–15). The integrity of moral sensibility and the verdict of the law must be harmonized. There are times when living by the letter of the law betrays the fidelity owed the divine author of morality.

The Myth of Absolute Immutability

What may be learned from the uneasiness felt by the Rabbis of tradition with those scriptural laws that appear to be morally tainted? What implications may be deduced from the midrashic episodes that inspire strong rabbinic challenges to divine laws? What kind of religious mind-set dared imagine God's sanctioning the revision of divine laws, including the nullification of some of God's own imperatives?

Contrary to the dogma of immutable divine law, the rabbinic practice of reinterpreting scriptural law indicates that the sages, explicitly or not, held change to be embedded in the Jewish tradition. Modification of biblical or rabbinic law is not something to be feared as alien or hostile to Judaism. To the contrary, the Rabbis in practice recognized the need to refine Jewish narratives and laws within the parameters of Jewish tradition. The Rabbis revered Torah but did not limit the definition of "Torah" to the canonized texts. Guided by moral reason, they interpreted the sacred text and expanded and enhanced its boundaries.

I suspect that the Rabbis of tradition faced the same apprehensiveness that contemporary rabbis confront: fear of the slippery slope. Change one law, circumvent, qualify, or negate one practice, and an avalanche of lawlessness will follow. Once change is accepted, what kind of permanence will faith and law hold? Moreover, if, as so many of the midrashic renditions of scripture indicate, God acknowledges the limitation of certain laws and is even willing to cancel divine decrees, what happens to the theological assertions that Torah laws are immutable and God impassible? I sense that the Rabbis of tradition acted on the belief that conscience is a potent instrument of change, and that the human capacity to change is a gift of God's love. God's flexibility, power to repent, and praise of human moral competence portray a God who is far from the implacable Master who must be obeyed slavishly by followers.

Moral Relativism

But if change is acknowledged and the mutability of divine law accepted, are we not reduced to an ethics of moral relativism? As the witticism has it, are the Ten Commandments but ten suggestions? Where is the unconditional character of God's categorical imperatives?

This is not a novel question facing men and women of modernity. The Rabbis of tradition recognized both the power of absolute commandments and its limitations. They confronted the moral dilemma of one absolute bumping into another. What happens, for instance, when the commandment to honor your father and mother collides with the commandment to keep the Sabbath? What happens when a parent asks his son, "Cook for me on the Sabbath"? Which absolute commandment—filial honor or fidelity to the Sabbath laws—is the child to obey? If the parent to be honored demands, contrary to biblical law, that his or her child not restore a lost animal, which obligation must give way to the other? Whatever the ruling, the unconditional character of the commandment is chipped away (B. Yevamoth 5b).

Consider the traditional Jewish principle of *pikuach nefesh*, the preservation of life, and the dilemma faced by those who must choose to observe that principle or the observance of the Sabbath. The Rabbis resolved that it is forbidden to delay any violation of the Sabbath should it stand in the way of saving the life of a person. They cited scripture (Lev. 18:5) regarding laws, "Which if a man do, he shall live by them," that is to say he shall not die by them. Thus the divine command of the Sabbath is to be superseded by the moral principle to save a human life. Moreover, those who would cling to the absolute of revering the Sabbath at the cost of endangering the life of the sick are the true heretics. In this context, Maimonides strongly contests:

> Hence you learn that the ordinances of the law were meant to bring upon the world not vengeance but mercy, loving-kindness and peace. It is of the heretics, those who assert that this is nevertheless a violation of the Sabbath and therefore prohibited, of them the Scriptures say, "Wherefore I gave them also statutes that were not good, and ordinances whereby they should not live." (Ezekiel 20:25)[6]

Keeping an absolute law that disregards life violates the moral purpose of the law. Here the observance of the absolute law, far from being a mark of reverence, perverts the law. What many dismiss as moral relativism, properly understood, may free absolute law from the yoke of obdurate inflexibility.

Consider further the absolute traditional religious principle that qualifies the duty to save an endangered life, even if that requires suspending the operation of all the commandments in the Torah. Three exceptions to saving your own life are made: no person may save his or her own life at the price of murder, adultery, or idolatry. But even these three exceptions are further qualified by the Rabbis. We are to ask, are the coerced decrees to commit idolatry or adultery intended to be performed as a public or as a private act? Is the coercion a royal decree motivated by ideological reasons or by personal pleasure? Is the decree meant to violate religion or to satisfy regal lust? (B. Sanhedrin 74a). Paradoxically, the absolute turns conditional. It depends on the

In the absence of actionable prosecution, only conscience remains to restrain the publicly invisible intentions of the unethical.

motivations of royal decree. If in private a Jew is ordered to "serve the idol and you shall not be killed," he should serve the idol and not be killed (B. Sifra 86b). Before a public venue, martyrdom is the proper stance. Distinctions must be drawn. Circumstances, conditions, and motivations must be taken into consideration in the execution of the law. Moral sensibility softens the rigidity of the absolute and weighs the consequences of inflexible living.

There are moral purposes behind the qualifications that allow exception to the unconditional rule. The Rabbis reasoned that the Torah said, "a man shall live through them," and not, "a man shall die through them" (cf. Yoma 85b). In the practiced rabbinic tradition, there is less concern with falling down a slippery slope than with falling into the hardening cement of absolute decrees. Absolutes live close to precarious precipices.

The Fear of God and the Fear of Torah

What kind of religious sensibility enabled the traditional sages to openly challenge God's words and God's will? The rabbinic sages prayed and observed Jewish law, studied the Torah intently, and feared God. But fear of God did not reduce them to muted acquiescence or intimidate them into unquestioning obedience. God was to be feared, but Torah was not to be feared. Pertently, the expression "fear of Torah" is nowhere mentioned in rabbinic literature, in contrast to the number of times the terms "fear of God" (*yirat elohim*), "fear of heaven" (*yirat shamayim*), and "fear of sin" (*yirat het*) are spread throughout Jewish liturgy and theology. Why no mention of "fear of Torah"? A number of Jewish scholars, among them Abraham Joshua Heschel, suggest that the absence of the term "fear of Torah" in Jewish religious literature is to caution us against setting too close an identity between Torah and God.[7] Such a parallelism between Torah and God might too readily lead to the deification of Torah, a bibliolatry that would prevent the believer from challenging any word of God. Not awe of Torah, but awe of God who gave the Torah, is the true apprehension.

Such distinctions between "fear of God" and "fear of Torah" are noteworthy. Once the "fear of Torah" is thought to be equivalent to the "fear of God," the text becomes untouchable, beyond the reach of human moral or rational criticism. If the awe of Torah and the awe of God were viewed as interchangeable, no biblical law could be challenged, much less superseded. When Torah is seen as the final word of God, no appeal can be made above the word of Torah. Who, fearing Torah, would dare question the edicts found in it or seek to alter divine words?

God is not Torah. God transcends Torah. God can be appealed to beyond the strictures of Torah. God can be moved and God's words can be changed. God is greater than the law. As we have seen, God can announce a verdict and have it revoked. "Fear of God" therefore supersedes "fear of law."

The Jewish understanding of the "fear of God" bears connotations different from other theological outlooks. For the nineteenth-century Christian theologian Søren Kierkegaard, "fear of God" suspends the ethical and leaps over ethics into the arms of the Commander. For Judaism, however, "fear of God" suspends the unethical command and liberates the believer from bondage to scriptural literalness. Paradoxically, it is the "fear of God" that frees the believer from the excesses of the "fear of Torah." Too close an identity of God and Torah stifles the critical conscience of human beings. "Fear of Torah" will bind us indiscriminately to the text, while "fear of God" may loosen the decree. "Fear of God" approaches Torah not as an immutable, inerrant set of laws that demand passive conformity, but as laws that may be measured by moral standards, at times resulting even in the annulment of divine laws.

For many, God and conscience are polar opposites, and to chose one is to surrender the other. In our view, fear of God is fear of self-betrayal, the betrayal of the self-gifted with moral judgment. To suppress conscience is to ignore the core of divine-human relationship. The proper fear of God is expressed in the love of moral conscience. Fear of God does not lead to mindless subservience, but to the exercise of compassionate intelligence. To fear God is to fear one's own moral cowardice. To fear God is to fear the human hardening of the heart. A conscienceless life fears no God.

What Is Meant by Conscience as "Fear of God"

As we have earlier noted, there is no biblical Hebrew word that translates "conscience." I propose that the biblical term that comes closest to the character and role of conscience is "fear of God" or *yirat elohim*. One of the earliest uses of "fear of God" in the Bible is found in the narrative of the two heroic Egyptian midwives, Shiphrah and Puah, who defied the edict of Pharaoh to kill all Hebrew male infants. By their acts of rescue, the midwives are explicitly said to "fear God" and are therefore rewarded by God, who establishes a household for them "because the midwives feared God" (Exod. 1:17, 21). The midwives' fear of God superseded their fear of Pharaoh's public edicts.

Scholars observe that whenever wrongful acts that carry no legal punishments appear in the Bible, *yirat elohim*, or the fear of God, is used. Nechamah Leibowitz maintains that "whenever the phrase 'Thou shalt fear thy God,' is used, it refers to the conscience of the individual." She concludes that in such cases beyond litigation, "only the individual conscience can know whether the action was committed in good or bad faith."[8]

When the Bible states, "You shall not curse the deaf nor place a stumbling block before the blind," the verse adds, "but you shall fear your God, I am the Lord" (Lev. 19:14). Why use the term "fear of God" in such cases? Perhaps because the deaf cannot hear the curses, nor the blind see those who place stumbling blocks before them. No auditory or visual witnesses can offer testimony against the whispered malediction or the malevolent placing of a stone before the sightless. The victims of such ethical violations are legally defenseless. There are no human courts to stay the hand of the trickster, nor policeman present to arrest the transgressors. In such cases, the arm of the law is short. In the absence of actionable prosecution, only conscience, or *yirat elohim*, remains to restrain the publicly invisible intentions of the unethical.

Conscience is the internal moral sense that remains when the formal conditions for halachic prosecution are absent. The rabbinic commentator Nachmanides warns of "scoundrels within the law" who look for loopholes in contracts and escape clauses from ironclad laws. Shrewdness may steal the mind of the naive. "He who holds out a cup of wine to the unsuspecting Nazarite, or offers the torn limb of a live animal to the unknowing, though not legally prosecutable, is morally culpable."[9] Law, biblical and rabbinic, can deal with transgressions in the public domain that are legally actionable. But in the realm of the private domain, punitive laws are mostly unenforceable. Dispositions of character, such as jealousy, scoffing, greediness, and quarrelsomeness, are not within the agenda of the court of justice. Yet, as Maimonides argued, such personal characteristics lie at the root of prosecutable sins such as fornication, robbery, and theft. He maintained that character faults are graver than other egregious acts because those addicted to such temperaments of character find it exceedingly difficult to give them up. As it is written, "Let the wicked forsake his ways, and the man of iniquity his thoughts" (Isa. 55:7).

Conscienceless dispositions not accessible to the prosecution of the law are as invidious as public violations of the law. The prophet Malachi defines those who have no "fear of God" as persons who live stealthy lives, practice sorcery, commit adultery, swear falsely, cheat laborers of their hire, or oppress widows, orphans, and strangers (3:5). These unprosecutable acts are discussed in Maimonides's *Laws of Repentance* (7:3), found in the *Mishneh Torah*, the Jewish code of law and ethics.

In the confessions of sins enumerated on Yom Kippur, the Day of Atonement, we focus on attitudinal defects that stand outside the parameter of the legal system, things such as impulsive thoughts, hardening of the heart, pride, and effrontery. These sins are beyond the reach of the law but within the reach of conscience. The sages of the Talmud (Berachoth 7a) held that "one pang of conscience is worth more than many lashes." As it is written, "A rebuke enters deeper into a person of understanding than a hundred strikes into a fool" (Prov. 7:10).

Matters of Temperament

If God is One and the revelation is one and the text is one, what accounts for the multiplicity and contradictions of interpretations? A midrash (*Pesikta de Rav Kahana, Piska* 12) presents a powerful analogy: God appears to people as a mirror. The mirror is one, but it reflects different images depending on the different types of personality that stand before it. According to the person's temperament, words are heard differently, the manna tastes differently, events appear differently. More than impersonal logic and objective scripture are involved in our human judgments. Temperament, the unarticulated and half-conscious disposition, plays a major role in our reflections. Temperament must be taken into account if we are to understand why certain verses light up and others are dim in our eyes; why some verses in the Bible or rabbinic midrashim are weighty while others are weightless.

The American philosopher William James drew attention to the importance of temperament in philosophy. In a bold statement he announced, "The history of philosophy is to a great extent that of a clash of temperaments." While such a sweeping statement may be exaggerated, it calls attention to the role of temperament in favoring our different attitudes toward the duty to obey and the duty to disobey. There are temperaments that are attracted to a structured tradition. They favor positions that tell them what, how, when, and where to believe and behave. Such temperament is correlated with the characteristics of passivity, acquiescence, and comfort with the security of "commandedness." Temperament is not sufficient to explain certain positions that are taken, but it clearly loads the evidence and biases the conclusion.

Beyond the edges of legalism and philosophy there are emotional temperaments that must be appreciated in order to understand the proclivities toward the culture of obedience and disobedience. The narratives surrounding the duty to disobey elicit pride in Jewish autonomy, assertiveness, initiative, and responsible activism. The duty to obey holds a strong grip on the longing for belonging, the yearning for community. Morris Raphael Cohen, the philosopher who repudiated supernatural religions, including Judaism, confessed the magnetic pull of ancient observances and found the celebration and commemoration of rites of passage a testimony to "the personal continuity with the spiritual tradition that is more eloquent than any phrase of my own creation."[10] Loving obedience to tradition is deeper and more sacred than personal invention. Sigmund Freud, himself no believer, confesses a tug of an invisible cord that is tied to "obscure forces and emotions, all the more powerful the less they were to be defined in words."

> However attractive the life of the private self, there is an intuitive sense that we cannot celebrate alone or mourn alone or be consoled alone. Laughter and tears call for community.

I am not alone in having come into contact with secular, atheist, and agnostic Jews who, notwithstanding their doubts and disbelief, express a yearning for the continuity, solidarity, and comfort of community. And community inevitably has its own laws, customs, and half-remembered rites of passage that help us grieve and be consoled, celebrate and commemorate. However

attractive the life of the private self, however stirring the stories
of rebellion, there is an intuitive sense that we cannot celebrate
alone or mourn alone or be consoled alone. Laughter and tears
call for community. And community depends on some willing
obedience to tradition. For most people, different dispositions
are interdependent, and both are found within community.

The differences of temperament and their influences on
our judgments play a considerable role in the tense exchange
between Rabbi Shimon ben Shetach, head of the Pharisees, and
the majority of rabbis in the Supreme Court of the Sanhedrin.
As reported in the Talmud (Sanhedrin 19a), the slaves of King
Alexander Yannai had killed a man and Rabbi Shimon summoned the king to appear before the tribunal. The king was
reluctant to attend, but Rabbi Shimon insisted. Turning to his
more conforming colleagues on the court, he urged them, "Set
your eyes boldly upon him and let us judge him." When the king
finally arrived, he sat himself on the chair and, owing to his legal
status, would not stand. Rabbi Shimon, addressing the king,
said, "Stand on your feet, King Yannai, and let the witnesses testify against you. It is not before us that you stand, but before
Him who spoke and the world came into being." The king
refused to stand, declaring that he would not accede to Rabbi
Shimon's order but only to the instructions of the other sages.
Rabbi Shimon turned to the right and the left, but his colleagues hid from his eyes and pressed their faces to the ground.
Saddened, Rabbi Shimon rebuked them sarcastically: "Are you
wrapped in thoughts?" Rabbi Shimon and the sages could each
cite scriptural and rabbinic precedence to rationalize their
responses, but beneath their arguments basic temperaments
and attitudes conditioned their decisions. Deciding when to
obey, whom to obey, and when to disobey involves conscience,
judgments of the mind, and temperaments of the heart.

3

CONSCIENCE AND COVENANT

Vertical and Horizontal

I make this covenant, with its sanctions, not with you alone, but both with those who are standing here with us this day before the Lord our God, and with those who are not with us here this day.

—DEUTERONOMY 29:13

The God of the Philosophers

Not all philosophies countenance the idea of covenant favorably. For Aristotle, the notion of a covenant between God and the human being is odd. "Will not the Gods seem absurd if they make contracts and return deposits and more?"[1] Aristotle's God enters no covenant. The self-sufficient God needs nothing and no one. The God of the philosophers is impassive, inaccessible to human pleading, and indifferent to human praise or petition. Between God and the human being, there is neither entreaty nor treaty. The eleventh-century Jewish philosopher Judah Halevi, in his *Kuzari*,[2] characterizes the implacable God of the philosophers as one that "neither benefits nor injures; and knows nothing about prayer, offerings, obedience and disobedience." Aristotle's God is the unmoved and unmovable magnet of the universe, in proper contrast with the Judaic idea of a God that is responsive to the praises and requests of human petitioners. The God of the Jewish covenant cares, listens, promises, rewards, intervenes, changes, and responds to human petition. The God of the Jewish covenant covets community. God's counsel to Adam, "It is not good for the human being to be alone" (Gen. 2:18), applies to God as well.

In Jewish thinking, the human cohort in the covenant is a "partner" with God. But what kind of parity is there between these partners? What boundaries limit the human partner and what boundaries, if any, surround God's will? May the human partner oppose God's command? Will God withdraw with silent anger or openly accept human critique?

The Duality in One Covenant

We are a covenanted people, but what kind of divine covenant is signified? Do the conversations between God and humans flow only from above to below, or from below to above as well? God and Israel are spoken of as covenantal partners, but are the cosignatories of the covenant equal or unequal partners? Is the covenantal relationship one of master and servant, or a more collegial one between teacher and student? In either case, the power and responsibility of each partner are not the same, since a servant does not engage in debate with a master in the same manner that a student may argue with a teacher.

The covenant is a marriage of interdependence that weds Israel to God. Though the covenant is one, it harbors two distinct and, at times, conflicting understandings of the stature and rights of the cosignatory partners. Two different religious temperaments coexist in the same covenant: a "vertical" one favoring a culture of assent that instructs dutiful obedience to the sovereign authority, and a "horizontal" temperament that is more open to a culture of dissent, inviting vigorous conversation between God and Israel. Each covenantal type projects differing dispositions toward the divine–human partnership. How the limits of partnership in the covenant are drawn reflect and affect the character of Jewish theology and Jewish ethics.

What boundaries limit the human partner and what boundaries, if any, surround God's will? May the human partner oppose God's command?

Until now I have drawn mostly upon midrashim that focus on the horizontal, or bilateral, orientation, because these confrontational, covenantal relationships are less studied and publicized and their ethical and theological implications are far less acknowledged. But both forms of covenant live together. We are concerned with how the vertical and horizontal covenant orientations coexist and how they manage the dialectic dynamic within the covenant.

Contrast, for example, the early biblical account of Abraham at Sodom with the later account of Abraham and the binding of Isaac. Abraham's responses to each of God's different imperatives reflect a distinct duality of attitudes toward the covenant. The two narratives of Abraham are separated by only three chapters in the Bible, but attitudinally they are far removed from each other. At Sodom, Abraham's questioning is morally assertive and judgmental: "Far be it from You! Shall not the Judge of all the earth deal justly?" (Gen. 18:25). Abraham is emboldened to challenge God's self-revealed character as "just and right" (Gen. 19). Justice and righteousness are the connecting virtues that enable the vigorous discussion between Abraham and God.

Not so the Abraham who dutifully obeys the command to place Isaac on the altar. Here, the divine–human engagement presupposes the attitudes of the unilateral, vertical covenant. Sovereign command is given from on high and Abraham's

fidelity is tested and verified by his willing obedience to the
Commander. In his reverential obeisance, Abraham has passed
God's test.

The two different types of relationship within the same
covenant foreshadow the moral and theological tension throughout the rabbinic tradition. Each type assigns a different weight
to the two agents of the covenant. Together, they reveal a more
balanced conception of Judaism.

The Vertical Covenant

The rabbinic metaphor that portrays the vertical covenant
depicts a sovereign God wielding a vault or cask over the heads
of the Children of Israel at the foot of Mount Sinai. Addressing
the people, God offers a conditional, either-or choice: "If you
accept the Torah, it is well; but if not, you will be buried on the
spot" (B. Avodah Zarah 2b). The choice is not subject to
debate. The human partner of the covenant is a subdued "silent
partner." Abraham understands that his duty is to do what he is
commanded. The metaphor of the vault from above is cast
down with tough love.

The vertical covenant is pronounced twice daily in the conditional proviso that accompanies the *Shema* prayer:

> If you earnestly heed the *mitzvoth*, I give you this day
> to love Adonai your God, and to serve God with all
> your heart and your soul, then I will favor your land
> ... take care, lest you be tempted to stray and to wor-
> ship false gods, for then, Adonai's wrath will be
> directed against you. (Deut. 6:4–9)

Although obedience to authority is the proper stance of the
faithful, dissent bears the stigma of rebellion. Throughout the
liturgical tradition, the unilateral covenant is predominant. At a
funeral, for example, when the justification of God (*tziduk ha-
din*) is recited, the bereaved is muted. "Who dares say what doest

Thou ... we know, Lord, Thy judgment and right, Thy decrees just and Thy judgment pure. None shall presume to question Thy judgment."[3] Death is a divine judgment that a true believer will not challenge. The Lord gives and takes, issues decrees and judges in truth. In Psalm 90:7–11, one of the traditional prayers recited at funerals, the aggrieved appeals to God in the tones of total submissiveness: "You, God, set out our sins before You, our secrets before Your presence ... who can know the power of Your anger, who can measure the reverence due to You?"

Although God's anger and intimidation in such prayers may prove disturbing to some, they presented no vexing problem for my Orthodox grandfather. My *zayde* neither expected personal ecstasy nor inspiration from his prayers. The rightness of the psalm in justifying God's verdict was never doubted. It only intensified his belief in the discipline of the vertical treaty, in which prayer is ordained and to be obeyed without question.

Zayde prayed by heart while simultaneously thumbing the pages of the Talmud. Asked how he could both pray and study at the same time, Zayde appeared perplexed by the question. For him, prayer was a *chov*, a debt owed to the Master of the Universe, a debt to be prayed off in three daily installments— *shacharit*, *minchah*, and *maariv* (morning, afternoon, and evening prayers). Debts must be paid. Inner intention or rationale is laudatory but ultimately discretionary.

Zayde prayed vertically. He modeled his understanding of worship along the lines of classic Talmudic texts. One such text proscribes the way to pray the nineteen benedictions of the *Amidah*, the central prayer of the Jewish liturgy: "A man must never petition for his request, even in the first three benedictions or in the last three benedictions, but only in the middle ones." In the first benediction, the worshiper resembles a servant addressing a eulogy to his master; in the middle benediction, the worshiper resembles a servant pleading for largesse from his master; in the last benediction, the worshiper resembles a servant who has received whatever his master grants

him, and the servant takes his leave (Berachoth, 34a). In vertical
covenant, a servant neither criticizes nor doubts the master, but
merely holds his tongue, praises his master, and obeys. The unilateral, vertical covenant summons up an acquiescent religious
temperament.

In a vertical covenant, should the human partner exceed
his bounds, the dialogue between him and God is curtly broken
off. The Talmud (Menachoth 29b) states that when Moses,
shown the future and moved by the piety of the second-century
rabbinic scholar Akiba, asks God why he, Moses, was chosen by
God, and not Akiba, God responds sharply, "Be silent. Thus it
has seemed to Me." When Moses is further shown what happens
to Rabbi Akiba, whose body is flayed and flesh weighed in the
meat market by the Romans, he asks, "Is such the reward for
Akiba's piety?" God again answers sharply: "Be silent! So it has
seemed to Me."

In a similar passage in the Midrash (Num. Rabbah 9:8),
when Rabbi Yochanan ben Zakkai protested the Roman mas-
sacres of his people, God retorts, "The Holy One has issued a
decree, and no one can question His decrees." God's decree is
the final word of the vertical covenant. Human questioning dis-
rupts the vertical dialogue.

Statutes

Obeisance in the unilateral covenant is particularly pronounced in those laws said to be inaccessible to rational or
moral reasons. These statutes (*chukim*), such as the prohibition
against wearing clothing mixed of linen and wool (*shatnez*), the
biblically ordained ritual of the red heifer (which paradoxically
purifies the defiled and defiles the purified), and the prohibition against eating pork, demand unquestioned obedience to
the divine one who issues such arational commands. Although
speculative rationale for such practices may be tolerated, obedience to the statutes is all that is demanded.

The Talmudic sages ask who is nobler—someone who practices goodness because it is commanded or someone who practices goodness without being commanded. From the perspective of the vertical covenant, the person who obeys laws because they are commanded is nobler. As Rabbi Haninah concludes: "Greater is the reward of those who are commanded to perform good deeds, than of those who without being commanded perform good deeds" (Baba Kama 87a). Piety calls for obedience to authority, not the celebration of human autonomy.

Are there any limits, then, to the total obedience of the believer? If the halacha is unconditional, the duty to observe the law is indisputable. Thus, the distinguished Orthodox philosopher and talmudist Joseph B. Soloveitchik does not single out Abraham's pleading on behalf of the citizens of Sodom, as he does Abraham's submission before the altar of Isaac. In his submission, Abraham heroically sacrifices his moral sense and reason. Abraham, Soloveitchik explains, was "madly in love with God" and prepared to sacrifice not only his son but also his moral sensibility. Abraham's acceptance of this "absurd" edict of God calls for "*sacraficium intellectus.*" Abraham is praised by Soloveitchik precisely because "he ignores the logos and burdens himself in the law, whose rationale he cannot grasp." Soloveitchik explains:

> The man of faith ... is able to reach a point at which not only his logic of the mind but even his logic of the heart and of the will, everything—even his own "I" awareness—has to give in to an "absurd" commitment. The man of faith is "insanely" committed to and "madly" in love with God.[4]

Rabbi Soloveitchik echoes the view of the Christian existentialist philosopher Søren Kierkegaard, for whom "the suspension of the ethical" is an act of supreme devotion to the One who commands. For Soloveitchik, the true "knight of faith," one who has absolute faith in the commands ascribed to God, suspends

ethical rationale and therein proves his God-intoxicated piety.
Who dares pit human conscience against the absolute imperatives of God?

The Consolations of Obedience

Although the relationship of vertical covenant may appear harsh
to others, it offers a deep measure of consolation to the
bereaved and the guilty. To lie prostrate before the sovereign
God is to raise personal tragedy to higher meaning. So, too, guilt
is preferable to meaninglessness, and it is sometimes better to
accept blame for misfortune than to sever the hopeful but
unfathomable relationship with God. To best God in an argument on the grounds of fairness is a sorry victory when it thereby
loses the mysterious meaning of God's inscrutable ways. Better
pain with purpose than pleasure without meaning.

A character in T. S. Eliot's *The Cocktail Party* confesses to her
psychiatrist,

> I must tell you that I should really like to think
> there's something wrong with me, because, if there
> isn't, then there's something wrong with the world
> itself—and that's much more frightening, that
> would be terrible. So I'd rather believe there is
> something wrong with me that can be put right.[5]

God's world need not be righted. Instead, the world is to be
faulted and forgiven. To assign my loss to an act of amoral
nature is to trivialize tragedy. If death and suffering are simply
the pursuits of nature, personal anguish is sad but trivial. If
suffering and death are accidents of nature, pain is but a consequence of lack of wisdom. Job, at the end of his fierce dialogue
with God, shifts from a confrontational conversation with God
to one of mute acquiescence. As Maimonides observes, although
Job is good, nowhere is he described as wise. At the end,
Job clasps his hand over his mouth and declares, "Behold, I

am vile; what shall I answer You? I will lay my hand upon my mouth" (Job 40:4). The Joban dialogue is broken off. The dialogue ends in silence. Only God's soliloquy is heard.

The Horizontal Covenant of Conscience

If the vertical-unilateral covenant conjures up the metaphor of an intimidating mountain looming over the heads of the Children of Israel, the horizontal-bilateral covenant suggests a bridge that moves traffic in both directions. On this two-way thoroughfare, the commandment may be questioned in the name of conscience.

In one of his autobiographical fragments,[6] the Jewish philosopher Martin Buber describes an exchange with an observant Jew who asked Buber whether he believes in the Bible. When Buber tells him that he does believe in the Bible, the observant Jew probes Buber's fidelity. The latter cites the biblical narrative in which the prophet Samuel angrily informs King Saul that his dynasty will be taken from him by divine judgment because Saul spared the life of King Agag, the conquered prince of Amalek. Agag, the tribal enemy of Israel, was to be killed, but King Saul disobeyed that divine order. When the heathen Agag approached the prophet Samuel, pleading, "Surely the bitterness of death is passed" (1 Sam. 15:32), Samuel hewed Agag to pieces and took away the kingdom of Saul. "Do you believe that?" the observant Jew asked Buber. Buber replied, "I have never been able to believe that this was a message of God. I do not believe it." The observant Jew responded, "What is it then that you do believe?" Buber answered, "I believe that the prophet misunderstood God." Buber's moral conscience would not sanction the merciless conduct of Samuel, and he

> Conscience is not inborn. Its potentiality is cultivated by parents, teachers, religion, and the collective conscience of a community.

therefore understood that Samuel must have misheard God's command.

In the course of this exchange, Buber reports that the observant Jew agreed with him. Buber commented that there was nothing astonishing in the fact that an observant Jew, "when he has to choose between God and the Bible, chooses God." Here, for the observant Jew, conscience, or the "fear of God," preempted the "fear of the Bible." Far from being disrespectful of the Torah, the "fear of God" insists that there are times when out of respect for God's justice and mercy, certain verses ought not be blindly followed.

Ernst Simon, educator, philosopher, and close friend of Martin Buber, also described the divine commandment as an echo of God's word. Nevertheless, Simon would not surrender his moral autonomy to the divine Commander. "Were someone to demonstrate to me that the oral law understands the commandment 'not to kill' as a prohibition against the killing of Jews by Jews alone, I would not accept this explanation of the commandment, and I would rely on my autonomy."[7] Simon's morality is rooted in the sense of conscience inherent in the bilateral-horizontal covenant.

Legends of Conscience

Martin Buber defined conscience as "that court within the soul which concerns itself with a distinction between the right and the wrong, and proceeds against that which has been determined as wrong."[8] How is that court within the soul acquired? Is conscience an innate power, a gift inherent in human nature, or is it acquired through community? For example, what court within the soul enabled the pagan king Abimelech to accuse God of immoral threats against him because he had sought intimate relations with Abraham's wife Sarah? This is manifestly unfair, Abimelech cried, for it was Abraham himself who introduced Sarah as his sister. He cries out, "O Lord, will You slay people, even though innocent?" (Gen. 20:4). Abraham used the same words to cry out against God's intention to destroy the whole of Sodom and Gomorrah (Gen. 18:23). Now it is the pagan king Abimelech who accosts Abraham for the deception that led him to the brink of adultery, saying, "You have done to me things that ought not to be done" (Gen. 20:9). Conscience is not the exclusive provenance of Israel.

Is conscience the "image of God" breathed into Adam's nostrils at birth, or a quality taught and transmitted by a culture? To what extent conscience is inborn or passed down is open to debate, but I am inclined to believe that conscience is not a matter of genes and chromosomes. Conscience is not inborn. Its potentiality is cultivated by parents, teachers, religion, and the collective conscience of a community. Moral sensibilities are formal, sensitized, and reinforced by the epic stories of a community. In the following biblical narratives, we see how the collective conscience of Judaism was honed.

First, the prophet Nathan discovers the cruel ruse that King David used to satisfy his lust for the married Bathsheba, plotting to have her husband, Uriah the Hittite, killed in battle. The intrigue discovered, Nathan confronts David with an incisive parable: There were two men in the same city, one rich and one poor. The rich man had large flocks and herds, but the poor man had only one ewe lamb that he had bought. He tended it and it grew up together with him and his children. One day, a traveler came to the home of the rich man, who was loath to take anything from his own flocks or herds to prepare a meal for the traveler. The rich man slaughtered the poor man's lamb and prepared it for his guest.

Hearing this account, David flew into a rage and declared, "The man who did this deserves to die." Nathan pointed his finger at David and spoke two Hebrew words that resonate throughout Jewish conscience: "*Atah ha-ish.*" "That man is you." The dormant conscience of the king was awakened. King David fasted, confessed his guilt, and repented. Such is the power of the prophetic conscience to touch David's "fear of God."

In a similar vein, the Bible tells of King Ahab, who coveted
the vineyard of Naboth and falsely accused him of apostasy and
disloyalty to the crown. Naboth stood trial against Ahab's false
witnesses and was stoned to
death, after which the king took
possession of the vineyard. The
prophet Elijah learned of this
and confronted Ahab with a
question spoken with three
Hebrew words that resonate
throughout the Jewish culture

> **Compassion without courage is an ephemeral sentiment; courage without compassion is a blind tiger.**

of conscience: "*Haratzachta v'gam yarashta?*" "Have you murdered, and will you inherit?" Ahab is taken aback. "So you have
found me out, my enemy?" Elijah responded, "Yes, I have found
you because you have committed yourself to doing what is evil in
the sight of the Lord." Elijah's stance struck the moral conscience of the king, who then fasted, lay himself in sackcloth,
and walked about subdued (1 Kings 21).

Both Nathan and Elijah defied the powers of royalty and
risked being sent to their death. There is a heroism in this sort
of conscience, a courage that carries risk. Conscience, while
wise and compassionate, is neither cognitive nor effective
alone. To know is not yet to act. To feel is not yet to do. To pray
is not yet to perform. Conscience stiffens the spine and allows
us to stand proudly before the threats of bribery, wealth, and
royalty. Conscience pleads the cause of the weak who are
wronged.

The prophet Jeremiah describes the knowledge of God in
behavioral terms.

> Did not your father eat and drink and do justice
> and righteousness, then it was well with him. He
> judged the causes of the poor and needy, then it
> was well. "Is this not to know Me?" says the Lord.
> (Jer. 22:15–16)

To know God is to act out in life the moral predicates of godliness. The duty of conscience is to "seek justice, undo oppression, defend the fatherless, plead for the widow" (Isa. 1:17).

Conscience resonates in the legends and stories of the Jewish people. These are the sorts of narratives that shape the collective conscience of faith, compassion, and courage. Compassion without courage is an ephemeral sentiment; courage without compassion is a blind tiger. Conscience is neither contemplation nor romantic sentiment, but a fusion of mind, heart, hand, and spine.

The duty to obey and the duty to disobey inform the covenant with contrasting attitudes. The duty to obey inclines toward a more stringent, absolutistic discipline that brooks no question of the divine Commander. Consequently, it offers greater certainty, safety, and security to the believer, and distances itself from the challenging postures predicated on the prerogatives of human conscience. The duty to disobey is more open to a reciprocal dialogue in which human conscience enjoys high status and encourages initiative and responsibility. Each perspective within the tradition engages the other with a temperamental and intellectual set of presuppositions that affect Jewish theology, ethics, and law. The character and power of each partner of the covenant are shaped by the two different versions of the covenant.

4

AGAINST CONSCIENCE

Cynicism is idealism gone sour.
—WILL HERBERG

Sharp-eyed social critics throughout the ages have questioned whether we should have conscience intrude in our public and private lives. Dostoevsky's Ivan Karamazov opens his heart to his saintly brother Alyosha in the poem of the Grand Inquisitor, and declares that "nothing is more seductive for man than his freedom of conscience, but nothing is a greater cause of suffering."[1] For all the public adulation of freedom of conscience, people would privately sell it for a mess of pottage. Dostoevsky argues that what men desire are three powers: "Miracle, Mystery, and Authority," and they would rather follow these powers than exercise freedom of conscience. Throughout history, men willingly turn over their freedom of conscience to another.

Ivan asks, "Who can rule man, if not he who holds their conscience in his own hands?" Submission to authority, bowing to mystery, and kneeling before magic are the tried pathways that bring the joys of freedom. Obedience, submissiveness, and surrender are the well-trodden roads to happiness. Talk of freedom of conscience and surrender to authority characterize "the absurdity of the human contradictions."

The contradiction between freedom of conscience and the stability of power is born out in the biblical tradition. In the Book of Genesis, when famine strikes Egypt, its citizens willingly relinquish their money, livestock, and finally their own freedom for the security that the state has promised. Men gratefully lay their freedom at the feet of Joseph, the vizier of the Pharaoh, and plead with him to buy their land in order to be bondsmen to Pharaoh. Willingly, they surrender their freedom and gratefully declare, "You have saved our lives. Let us find favor in the sight of my Lord and we will be Pharaoh's bondsmen" (Gen. 47:25).

Freed from the oppression of Pharaoh, the Children of Israel would forego their emancipation for the leeks, cucumbers, garlic, and fish doled out to them by their Egyptian masters (Num. 11:5). Better security than freedom; better subservience to authority than deliberation of conscience. The Bible describes a slave who is about to be emancipated, and yet declares his love of his master, pleading to remain under his dominion. The subservient slave is taken by the ear—the same ear that once heard the divine voice of God who took him out of bondage—and allows himself to be pierced and then branded as if he were a domesticated animal (Exod. 21:5–6; Deut. 15:17). This implies that freedom on an empty stomach is no match for a mess of pottage.

> Who are we when we are undetected? When the doors are closed, the windows shut, and no witness or police is to be found, the selfish hidden self surfaces.

When Moses the liberator disappears from view, the emancipated Children of Israel quickly fall apart. They need someone, anyone, to choose for them, guard them, and lead them. They demand of Aaron, the priest, to build them an altar and "Make us a God" (Exod. 32:1). They rise to offer burnt offerings and peace offerings to the golden calf, and sit down to eat and drink and make merry. Mystery, magic, and authority, not liberty, freedom, or the powers of conscience, are the inner yearnings of the heart. From the story of the golden calf, we learn that idealization of conscience masks the true idolatrous craving of humanity.

The Myth of Gyges

Glaucon, one of the pugnacious sophists in Plato's *The Republic*, smiles contemptuously at Socrates's efforts to convince others that the life of honesty and justice and conscience yield authentic happiness and that only a life of virtues will bring true contentment. Glaucon rips off the mask of conceit and reveals the deceitful inner motivation of conscience and the truth about human nature. Glaucon presents Socrates with the following parable that exposes what lurks beneath conscience.

Gyges, a shepherd in the service of the king of Lydia, comes upon a cave that has been opened by a terrible storm. Gyges enters the cave and sets his eyes upon a man of stature wearing a gold ring. The man is dead. Gyges removes the ring and discovers that when he turns the ring one way he becomes invisible, and when he turns the ring the other way he becomes visible again. Tempted by this new power, Gyges makes himself invisible, seduces the queen, slays the king, and robs the palace of its treasures. Invisible, Gyges acts out of his true nature, his real desires liberated from the fine cloak of public respectability. With the turning of the ring, his conscience has turned invisible. For Glaucon, conscience is only the fear of being caught.

Who are we when we are undetected? Where is conscience when men are anonymous? When the doors are closed, the windows shut, and no witness or police is to be found, the selfish hidden self surfaces. As the sociobiologist M. T. Ghiselin quipped, "Scratch an altruist and watch a hypocrite bleed."[2]

Freud: The Truth about Human Nature

Sigmund Freud, master of the human psyche, understands the
depth of the myth of Gyges. He writes:

> The bit of truth behind all this [talk of virtue]—
> one so eagerly denied, is that men are not gentle,
> friendly creatures wishing for love, but that a pow-
> erful desire for aggression has to be reckoned
> with as part of that instinctual endowment. The
> result is that their neighbor is only to them not
> only a possible helper or sexual object, but also a
> temptation to them to gratify their aggressiveness
> on him, to exploit his capacity for work without
> recompense, to use him sexually without his con-
> sent, to seize his possessions, to humiliate him, to
> cause him pain, to torture and to kill him; *homo
> homini lupus*—who has the courage to dispute it in
> the face of all the evidence in his own life, and in
> history?[3]

The noble rhetoric about conscience, love, compassion, self-
sacrifice, and altruism are the disguises of human hypocrisy. In
Freud's thinking, the predatory origins of man's personality are
natural and instinctive. The moral overlay of civilization is con-
trived. Freud's is a secular version of Augustine's original sin.
Man is "foul and crooked, sordid, rotten, bespotten and ulcer-
ous." Freud's portraiture of human nature is etched in the acidic
words of the playwright Tennessee Williams:

> The only difference between man and other beasts
> is that man is a beast who knows that he will die …
> the only honest man is an unabashed egoist … the
> significant ends of life are sex and money, so the
> human comedy is an outrageous medley of lechery,
> alcoholism, homosexuality, blasphemy, greed, bru-
> tality, hatred and obscenity.[4]

The American philosopher of naturalism, George Santayana, offers a slightly gentler version of human nature. He writes, "In human nature, generous impulses are occasional or reversible." The generous responsibility that is spent in childhood dreams is often "soured in old age."[5] Santayana concurs with Freud. Scratch the patina of altruistic sentiment, and lurking beneath it we find base motivations—sex, money, and fame.

Nietzsche: The Craftiness of Conscience

Friedrich Nietzsche, the philosophic hammerer of the late nineteenth century, finds more than hypocrisy in the public paens to conscience. For him, conscience is the sleight of hand by which the weak and powerless surreptitiously emasculate the strong and noble. The slave shrewdly slips into the citadel of the powerful, pleading pity and compassion in order to soften the braver heart of the master. Sheep bleat and sparrows chirp cries of mercy so as to extract claw, beak, and bite from the arsenal of the strong. Conscience is the crafty weapon of the slave by which he controls the master.

The slave is no more virtuous than the master. Jealous of the master's domination, the slave resents the master, whose whip he would like to hold. With guile, the weak prey upon the powerful in order to loosen the grip of the master's hand and transfer it to their own hand.

In his *Geneology of Morals*,[6] Nietzsche pays Jews and Judaism a back-handed compliment. Because they shrewdly labeled the weak "strong" and the strong "weak," the Jewish priests knew how to turn Israel's misfortunes into gentile guilt. Jewish "slave morality" twists conscience into a toxin paralyzing the powerful. Oppressed, the Jews took revenge on their masters by fueling the resentment of the weak against the strong:

> All the world's efforts against the aristocrats, the
> mighty, the holders of power are negligible by

> comparison with what has been accomplished
> against those classes by the Jews—that priestly
> nation, which eventually realizes that the only
> method of effecting satisfaction on its enemies and
> tyrants was by means of a radical transvaluation of
> values, which was at the same time their cleverest
> revenge.[7]

According to Neitzsche, conscience is the revenge of the impo-
tent, who manage to invert the aristocratic value equations of
good and nobility, power and prosperity. For the underprivi-
leged, a clever inversion of values is introduced. "Only the poor,
the powerless are good; only the suffering, sick and ugly are
truly blessed." The punitive pangs of conscience are but the
"sour grapes" of the effete. Conscience is exploited by the slave
so that he can sit in judgment over the master. The master, to
retain his superiority, should guard against the subversive voice
of conscience.

Social Darwinism and Conscience

Much in the tenor of the Nietzschian critique of conscience,
Social Darwinists such as William Graham Sumner and Herbert
Spencer denigrate the virtues of compassionate conscience.
Both find moral conscience and its associated virtues deleterious factors in the ascent of man. According to Social Darwinism,
conscience inhibits the wisdom of evolutionary natural selection
and denies the survival of the fittest. In nature, the weak are
properly weeded out and the inferior fall by the wayside. We
would be wiser to imitate nature's ways. What happens to a sow
that has a runt in the litter? She eats it. What happens to a muta-
tional baby chick? The mother pecks it to death. What happens
to wolves who go on a hunt? The injured and slow-footed among
them are soon abandoned. Contrary to the ways of nature,
human governments foolishly build asylums for the sick, offer

welfare to the incompetent, protect the talentless, and extend the lives of the incapacitated. Human interventions in society destroy the wisdom of natural evolution and prove injurious to the race of man.

In his essay on population,[8] Thomas Malthus similarly disapproved of relief for the poor. War, disease, and poverty are natural antidotes to the rapid explosion of the population. Tamper with nature and the fittest will fall to the side. Attend the voice of conscience and our economy will be drained and our energy exhausted. Such is the formula for the survival of the unfittest.

Herbert Spencer exposes the case history of one woman called Margaret, a "gutter child" who was supported by government welfare. Because of such foolhardy benevolence, Margaret proves to be a "prolific mother of a prolific race." The records of the courts of New York showed that 200 of Margaret's descendants were idiots, imbeciles, drunkards, lunatics, paupers, and prostitutes. Spencer asks rhetorically, "Was it kindness or cruelty which generation after generation enabled these to multiply and become an increasing curse to the society around us?"[9]

> Attend the voice of conscience and our economy will be drained and our energy exhausted. Such is the formula for the survival of the unfittest.

Victorian era Social Darwinists such as Spencer used evolutionary theory to justify colonialism and imperialism, opposition to labor unions, and withdrawal of aid to the sick and needy. They argued that moral sympathy for the suffering of fellow human beings runs against the grain of nature. Compassionate conscience perverts the natural cunning of evolution. Conscience does not choose the blessings of life; it only invites the curse of degeneracy.

Contrary to the Social Darwinists, however, Darwin himself took no such morbid view of the role of morality and conscience in evolution. He writes: "Any animal whatsoever endowed with well-masked social instincts, the parental and filial affection being here included, would inevitably acquire a moral sense of conscience."[10]

Theological Suspicions

The theologians insist that God's goodness is not humanity's. Humanity's autonomy is ensnared in self-interest. Who can trust the conscience of fallible, errant human beings who justify their selfish aims? Who would depend on human rationality? Some theologians conclude that our choice is either between uncompromising faith in the divine command or fallible human sensibilities. The Protestant theologian Karl Barth spelled out the consequences of such a choice:

> Either we hear it as the command of His goodness (even though it is a command to shoot) or we do not hear it at all (even though it commands us to preach). Either we obey it in the unity which it is always and everywhere true and valid ... or we do not obey it. Either we love or do not love.[11]

The Jewish theologian Abraham Joshua Heschel assumes a similar stance. He asserts that "ultimate standards are beyond man, rather than within man." For Heschel and many defenders of the evident superiority of faith over conscience, the latter is "not capable of teaching us what we ought to do, but a preventive agency." At best, Heschel writes, "conscience is a brake, not a guide; a fence, not a way."[12] Which voice should the faithful heed: God's will or human moral judgment, divine dogma or human conscience? Heschel avers that "God's will stands higher than man's creed." Such theological arguments choose dependence on the divine command over reliance on autonomous conscience. What rational person would follow man's fallible ethical ideals and turn from the inerrancy of God's commandment?

Such a theological argument, however, begs the questions: How do mortals know the quality of the command, or the source of the command, or whether the command is just and righteous? How do errant souls know whether the law comes cast from above in pristine form, unfiltered by human transmitters and their self-interest? Whether from heaven or from earth, the word must ultimately be measured by the rod of moral sense. Throughout history and in our times, we have witnessed too many faiths eager to do the "will of God" and surrender to God's inscrutable and immutable word, only to end up justifying persecution, torture, maiming, and murder. Voices from heaven must not be given a blank check to be filled in by claims to be the "will of God." If, as Heschel puts it, conscience is at most only a brake, it is nevertheless a brake on both the wheels of heaven and the wheels of earth. Any authority or any text, whatever claim is made of their divine source, needs to be subject to moral evaluation.

Although conscience may be dismissed as merely human, it is nevertheless all we humans have. If we abandon our moral competence and surrender our freedom of conscience to an alleged divine Commander, we are reduced to automata. If the human crown of God's creation is defamed, God has failed to create us in God's own image. A conscienceless creature is a slave, and God does not create slaves. If conscience is a fence, it is erected to protect the gullible from succumbing to all forms of totalitarianism, religious as well as political.

It is of course a risk to listen to your conscience, but no less a risk than to listen to the commanding voice of faith. As Buber declares, "Moloch imitates the voice of God."[13] By what measure can we discern the difference between the voice of God and the ventriloquism of Mephistopheles except by examining the content of the command? To have faith in faith alone is to abandon the difference between good and evil. Moral differentiations are of the sort to rely on the discernment of conscience.

One of Dostoyevsky's characters famously declares, "If there is no God, everything is permissible." Yet, examining history, may we not more properly conclude that if there is a God, everything is permissible? The critical issue is not whether God is believed but rather what kind of God is believed. Satan believed in God but did not love or understand God. Stripped of conscience, Satan embraces any power, good or evil. Everything therefore depends on the kind of God believed in and the kind of commandment that is demanded. And how are we to know God or commandment except through the moral yardstick of conscience?

Some consider moral conscience to be a revelation of godliness. But conscience is itself not exempt from critique. The duty to question and to disobey authority applies to the rebel as well as to the believer. All claims are open to the critique of motivation and consequence.

Judaism: The Morality of Theistic Humanism

The bias against conscience strikes at the heart of Jewish theology and anthropology. The strong conviction in the moral potentiality of the human being to share with God the responsibility for the world's survival and improvement is basic to Judaism. The human is co-creator. The world is not made of milk and honey, and human beings are fragile and fallible. Even so, the psalmist believes in human moral competence, responsibility, and the active power to shape history: "You have made man but little lower than God [*Elohim*]. You have made man master over your handiwork" (Ps. 8:5).

Jewish theistic humanism is a theme that runs throughout the biblical and rabbinic tradition. Consider the rabbinic commentary on a biblical verse that warns that allowing a condemned criminal to "hang all night is a reproach of God" (Deut. 21:22). The commentator asks why such an act is regarded by the Bible as a reproach to God. Rashi, the eleventh-century commentator, answers the query with an audacious analogy based on Deuteronomy 21:22: The meaning of the biblical verse may be likened to the twin brother of a king, who became a bandit and was condemned and hanged for his crime. People viewing the hanged body of the twin brother might mistake him for the king. In this parable, God and man are, as it were, twins: God is the king and his twin brother the human being. The Bible calls the exposed body of man a "reproach to God" because the humiliation of a human being is a desecration of God's twin. The hanging of a human being defiles God's crown of creation.

In the *Brothers Karamazov*, one of Dostoevsky's characters explains, "I don't accept the world of God. It is not that I don't accept God, but the world created by Him I cannot accept." To be a believing Jew is to believe in God and accept God's created world. The Jew cannot accept God and abandon the world. To be a Jew is to be bound to this world and pledged to repair and sanctify it. In the rabbinic text, *Ethics of the Fathers*, the dignity and responsibility of God's partner is summed up aphoristically: "Better one hour of repentance and good deeds in this world than the whole life in the world to come" (4:21).

The duty to question and to disobey authority applies to the rebel as well as to the believer.

Yet, with all due respect for the theistic moral humanism in Judaism, who can deny Freud's bleak metapsychological view of human nature? Scripture, prophesies, and rabbinic citations may eulogize the human being, but who can look at the pyramids of shoes, the skeletal remains, the mass graves, the green and yellow smoke rising toward the skies, and find goodness in humankind? Knowing of the Holocaust's decimation of 11 million souls—including the 1.5 million children slaughtered because they were Jews, two of every three Jews in Europe, one of every three Jews in the world murdered—who can wave aside Nietzsche's ridicule of Jewish optimism, "to regard nature as if it were proof of the goodness and care of God and to interpret history as enduring testimony to the moral order and ultimate purpose of the world—such view is no longer tenable: it has conscience against it"? Conscience testifies against belief in the goodness of God's world.

In light of what we know of the genocidal cruelty and baseness of human beings, who can with a straight face view human nature as a manifestation of God's image? Is talk of conscience not the speech of hypocrisy? Is there a shred of empirical evidence to counter the verdict of human bestiality? Are there any credible witnesses of men and women who exercised the powers of their moral conscience?

The prophet Isaiah spoke to his people in God's name: "'You are My witnesses,' declares the Lord, 'and I am God'" (Isa. 43:13). The sages interpreted God's declaration to mean: "When you are My witnesses, I am God, but when you are not My witnesses, I am, as it were, not God" (Midrash, Psalm 123:1). Where are the witnesses to be found, and if there are none, where is the nobility of conscience to be found?

5

WITNESS TO GOODNESS

"Unto Thee, O Lord, do I lift up my eyes, O Thou that sittest in the heavens (Psalm 123:1)." This implies that when I do not lift up my eyes, Thou wouldst not be sitting in the heavens.

—MIDRASH TEHILLIM ON PSALM 123:1

Following Freud's tough-minded rendition of human nature, it seems easier to find witnesses to Satan's malevolence than empirical testimony to God's goodness. Consider the witnesses for the prosecution. Genocide punctuates our history. The first genocide of the twentieth century began in 1915 when the Ottoman Turks massacred 1.5 million Armenians. Denial enveloped the world. The Nazis organized deliberate and disciplined plans and exterminate 6 million Jews and 5 million non-Jews in the Shoah. The world was stricken mute. Under Stalin's regime, 3 million POWs and 2 million Poles were liquidated, and 20 million Russians were murdered. The world was eyeless. Mao Zedung's policies resulted in the death of 30 million of China's own citizens. Voices were suffocated. The Communist Khmer Rouge murdered 1.7 million of its own people in Cambodia. Silence hovered over the face of the killing fields. Saddam Hussein's Baath party destroyed 100,000 Kurds in Iraq. The civilized world held its tongue. In 1994, 800,000 Rwandans were annihilated in one hundred days, and three-quarters of the Tutsi population were destroyed. Desultory attention was paid. In the first genocide of this new century, close to 400,000 of the people of Darfur in Sudan have been tortured, tormented, and killed, and 2.5 million of them have been displaced, their homes torched. Silence again strangles the voice of conscience.

Who can deny the sad litany of Freud, Nietzsche, Santayana, and others who can call so many witnesses to testify to the ugliness of human nature? Each year Satan gains more allies to nefarious causes than God attracts cohorts to benevolent designs.

Heschel, addressing teachers, once declared, "If you ask me how to begin teaching children the conception of God, I would tell you to begin by teaching the conception of human nature."[1] But how is faith in God to be taught through human nature when it is easier to believe in God than to believe in humanity? How will the teaching of human nature bring children closer to God? If we teach them the chilling statistics, will their hearts not freeze over? Will the benevolence of God be taught through the devastating knowledge that among all the children of the world, 150 million are dangerously malnourished and 30,000 die each day from preventable diseases? As for their parents, 22 percent of the world population lives below the poverty line, 841 million suffer from malnutrition, and 800 million endure without access to medical care.[2]

Contemporary history mocks a theology that trumpets God's reflected image in humanity. History ridicules the conceit of conscience.

We are caught in a double-bind: Should we tell our children the hideous truth, or should we hide from them the acts of human atrocity? Should we let them know the horrors of human nature, or should we shut off their television so that they cannot see the daily pornography of callousness and cruelty? Dare we show them the emaciated faces of children on whose eyeballs infectious flies dance a choreography of disease and death, while the children are too weak to wave them away? Can we, in the face of the darkness of human nature, eulogize God and offer songs to the human crown of creation?

We are trapped in an unyielding vise—to lay a heavy stone upon the heart of children or to rob them of the truth. Cicero observed, "Not to know what happened before you were born is to remain a child forever." Children must not be lied to. Ignorance is lethal. The infantalization of the young only renders them vulnerable to the demonic forces in the present and the future.

Not only is the child's morale jeopardized by the global terror, but our own adult faith is also shaken. The grim anthropology of Freud scatters the seeds of Jewish faith to the winds of despair. The world's depression cannot be denied.

Ben Gurion's Search for Morale

The prime minister of Israel, David Ben Gurion, sensed the internal tensions produced by the contradictions of fact and faith. In 1961 Adolph Eichmann, the mass murderer of Jews during the Nazi era, was put on trial in Jerusalem. The horrific testimony against Eichmann and his collaborators was so overwhelming that Ben Gurion feared it would traumatize the morale of the Jewish people, and yet the indifference of the world's bystanders troubled him as well. Would the mounting evidence of worldwide apathy create in the Jewish people the unbearable despair of a people abandoned? The prime minister was concerned with the people's depressed morale that might well follow the sordid testimony of hatred and world abandonment. He sought a few sparks of light to brighten the shadows of cavernous disillusion. In 1961 Ben Gurion urgently instructed the Holocaust Memorial at Yad Vashem to find and honor twenty-four non-Jews who saved Jews at the risk of their own

> History ridicules the conceit of conscience.

lives. In their memory, trees were planted in a garden that would become the Avenue of the Righteous.[3]

The sanity of a civilization depends on some evidence of human goodness. Evidence of moral conscience is critical for a fairer portrait of humankind and for a brighter prospect for civilization than the one drawn by Freud. It is not that Freud and the others were wrong in exposing the elements of exploitative sadism in humanity, but that they saw human nature with one eye closed. Freud's portrait of humankind is disfigured.

There were far more than twenty-four non-Jews who risked life, limb, and treasure to save Jews during the Holocaust. Tens of thousands of non-Jews, Christians, communists and atheists, from all walks of life—priests and farmers, diplomats and peasants, nuns and businessmen—jeopardized their lives and those of their families by issuing foreign passports and false baptismal papers to hide Jews from their tormented fate. These rescuers saved persons not of their liturgy or catechism. They risked their lives not for personal gain but out of moral conscience.

What would Freud say about such rescuers—some of whom I have met and many of whom I have learned about from those whom they rescued? What would Freud have to say of the documented exploits of the thousand of non-Jews who hid Jews in their homes, attics, or pigsties, carefully watched by Nazis and informers? What would Freud and the others say about the reality of human altruism after interviewing those rescuers who, when asked "Why?" answered simply, "What was there to do? What would you do? What would any human being do?"

I offer a number of vignettes of ordinary people who saved strangers at the risk of their lives and that of their families. I ask the reader, as I ask myself, why such documented stories of holy disobedience remain untaught, unheralded, unsung in churches, synagogues, and mosques. As Shakespeare asked, why does the "evil that men do lives after them, the good is oft interred with their bones" (*Julius Caesar*, act III, scene 2)? Why do adults and children of all persuasions know the names of Heinrich Himmler and Adolf Eichmann but nothing of heroic Christian and gentile rescuers like Alex Rozlan and Hermann Graebe? Why is villainy "Front Page" and moral heroism "Obituary"? Why is the heroic duty to disobey repressive authority not elevated among the virtues of the religious life?

Evidence of human decency and self-sacrifice during the Holocaust in no way mitigates the horrors of the killing camps. The tragedy of the Holocaust cannot be reversed. As the Talmudic sages put it, "Whoever prays to reverse what has already happened utters a 'vain prayer'" (Berachoth 54a). History is irreversible. Poet Dan Pagan writes, "You cannot turn the scream back into the throat or the gold teeth back into the gums or the yellow star back into the heavens." Still, human nature needs and ought to be freed from the paralyzing bias against man. The future of civilization rests upon a balanced view of humanity. Something important has been left out of the lopsided Freudian analysis of human nature.

To Discover Conscience in Hell

What link may be found between the conception of human nature and that of the nature of God? If the divine vine produces only sour grapes, will the children's teeth not be set on edge? The psalmist sings, "Taste and see how good the Lord is" (Ps. 34:9). But what if the taste is bitter? "Why," the psalmist cries, "do You hide Your face, ignoring our affliction and distress?" If the presence and goodness of God is to be found, it should be uncovered on earth. Where can we search for godliness among the ashes of Auschwitz?

When, in 1963, I founded the Institute of Righteous Acts (later lodged at the Judah Magnes Museum in Berkeley, California), I convinced my friend, psychologist Perry London, to interview some of the gentiles known to have risked life and limb to save Jews. Perry was my last resort. Earlier, I had approached faculty members in the sociology department at the University of California, Berkeley, to research the altruistic personality in the manner that social scientists had researched the authoritarian personality. Why was anti-Semitism alone the only subject worthy of scientific investigation? Why does philo-Semitism appear chimerical? Without exception, the members of the sociology department trivialized the notion of altruism. For them, the claims of altruism were disingenuous. Echoing Freud, they maintained that beneath the surface of conscience resides the baser motivations of sexual exploitation, economic greed, or the quest for publicity. The term *altruism*, coined by Auguste Comte in the nineteenth century, appeared late in our vocabulary. Altruism, both the word and the recognition of its virtue, comes late in the study of social science.

Twenty years after my unsuccessful efforts to place the acts of righteous Christians during the Holocaust on the Jewish agenda, I founded the Jewish Foundation for Christian Rescuers, now called the Jewish Foundation for the Righteous. The Foundation is dedicated to the study and recognition of the largely ignored phenomenon of Christian rescuers, and to raising funds to offer stipends to the largely ignored rescuers so that they may live out their waning years with some measure of dignity, recognition, and material help. The Foundation continues its work to give economic aid to close to 2,000 non-Jewish rescuers, all identified as such by those whom they saved. At its yearly dinner, the Foundation reunites a rescuer with the person he or she rescued.

In recent years, a number of scholarly books have gathered further testimony of this neglected phenomenon. I have culled from this new scholarship the documented illustrations of the grandeur of human conscience and have pondered over implications for the nature of God and human beings. What follows are real life testimonies to the redemptive power of conscience in parlous times.[4]

An Entire Village: The Conspiracy of Goodness

A number of years ago, at a Holocaust conference held in Washington, D.C., a Dutch rescuer approached me after my talk. I had spoken about the conspiracy of evil and argued that atrocity could not have been achieved without the collaboration of informers, blackmailers, and the not-so-innocent bystanders. The rescuer pointed out that I had said nothing about the conspiracy of goodness. He asked me if I thought that a hunted Jew could be concealed behind false walls or be fed and clothed without the tacit agreement of others. To help the rescued meant to lie to the hunters, to resist the bribes of a bottle of vodka or a carton of cigarettes, and to issue constant warnings about the designs of the predators. Human goodness in Nazi-occupied lands called for a conspiracy of men, women, and children of conscience.

He called attention to a major insight about the rescuers. There is a conspiracy of goodness in saving lives. Acts of individual conscience depend on the support of community.

Consider the Dutch village of Niewlander and the behavior of one of its Christian citizens, Arnold Douwes. Upon learning of the anti-Semitic measures introduced by the Nazis, Douwes could not rest until he did something to save the beleaguered Jewish refugees. His Dutch friend, Johannes Post, a farmer, also resolved to save Jews, a decision that involved neglecting his eight children and his farm.

Jews had been gathered to report to Westerbork en route to Poland and Germany. Few doubted their final destiny. Contacting the Dutch underground, Douwes provided the panic-stricken Jews with food and counterfeit identity papers. Even more impressively, Douwes did not act alone. He was part of a conspiracy of goodness. Every home in Niewlander, a total of several hundred Dutch families, took in at least one hunted Jew. There were no informers against their work in the village because everyone was implicated in the conspiracy of goodness.

Five hundred Jews, including one hundred children, were saved. Douwes's fellow co-conspirator, Johannes Post, had a price placed on his head and was eventually caught by the Nazis. Douwes himself was placed on the Gestapo's criminal list and was arrested in January 1945. While awaiting execution, he was freed by villagers in a daring raid. It takes a village to save a marked man, woman, or child. The entire village of Niewlander was awarded the designation of Righteous Among the Nations in 1987.

Are such heroic acts to be waived aside as mere aberrations of human nature, or can they help moderate the lugubrious conceptualizations of human nature? Do such rescuers not own an honored place in the fuller characterization of human nature?

Stefa Krawkowska: The Heroism of Hiding

The woman, however, had taken the two men and hidden them ... now she had taken them up to the roof and hidden them under stalks of flax, which she had lying on the roof.

—JOSHUA 2:4, 6

Stefa Krawkowska, a Polish peasant, hid fourteen Jews for a long period of time in a small attic built as a storage room. The attic had no toilet facilities, no water, no light—only a single pail shared by the fourteen Jews ranging in age from three and a half to sixty. Dirt, lice, and vermin lay over the cramped quarters in the attic. People had to be fed, and it was dangerous to bring them bread or potatoes, for the Nazi's had issued strict orders warning that those who helped Jews would pay with their lives. Many Poles did.

The people you hide grow sick and some die. How do you find medicine or a doctor for the imperiled under such circumstances? As Nechama Tec, a sociologist who investigated the relationship between the rescuers and the rescued, ironically comments, "How does one call a doctor for someone who does not exist? Or still, how does one bury a body that isn't there?"[5] One of the fourteen Jews hidden by Stefa Krawkowska was an old Jewish woman lying near death. The dying woman worried not as much about her death as about her burial: how would her body be buried without giving away the secret that there were people being hidden in the attic? To bury the body whole would reveal the secret of their location and activities and thus endanger other lives. The old woman whispered to Stefa, "My God, my body may bring disaster to you. What will you do with my body, how will you manage?" The old woman died. Late at night, secretly and in stages, they buried her dismembered body in Stefa's garden.

Where do Stefa and the old woman figure in the dark metapsychology of Freud and the denigration of sympathy and compassion of Nietzsche? Are these choices of conscience anomalies of human nature, or ought they figure significantly in a truer understanding of human nature?

Seven Sisters and a Mother Superior

A Benedictine nunnery stood close to the crowded Vilna ghetto, where Jews were humiliated and tortured. The mother superior, a graduate of Krakow University, was a young woman of thirty-five when Jews were driven from their homes. Hearing of their torment, she summoned the other nuns, who agreed to establish contact with the ghetto and formed an underground railroad to smuggle Jews out of the ghetto, bringing many into the nunnery itself. Out of nowhere, nuns with unmistakably masculine features appeared in black habits. Among those hidden in the convent were Jewish leaders of the ghetto uprising—Arie Wilna, Abraham Sutzkever, Edek Boraks, and Abba Kovner.

In the winter of 1945, a Jewish fighters organization was formed in the ghetto and the mother superior, assisted by other nuns, searched the country for knives, daggers, bayonets, pistols, guns, and grenades, which they smuggled into the hands of the Jewish resisters. As the writer Philip Friedman wryly observes in his pioneering book *Their Brothers' Keepers,* "Hands accustomed to the touch of rosary beads became experts with explosives."[6] The first grenades received by the Jewish fighters were the gift of the mother superior, who instructed them as to their proper use, inasmuch as the grenades were of a special brand unfamiliar to the fighters.

The mother superior spoke these words to Abba Kovner, a leading figure of the Jewish fighters:

> I wish to come to the ghetto to fight by your side, to die if necessary. Your fight is a holy one. You are a noble people. Despite the fact that you are a Marxist[7] and have no religion, you are closer to God than I.[8]

The mother superior recognized the conscience of an avowed atheist and the godliness that dwells within the secular. Conscience is the connective tissue that binds the religious and the secular. The sisters' holy disobedience supports the belief that the discipline of moral conscience transcends the boundaries of institutional religion.

Diplomat Rescuers

> *Who shall live and who shall die ... who shall perish by fire, and who by water, who shall rest and who shall wander?*
>
> —FROM THE HIGH HOLIDAY
> LITURGY—*UNETANEH TOKEF*

There are people who, with a piece of paper and a single stamp in hand, hold the awesome power to issue life or death sentences. They have in their hands the choice to avert the evil decree.

Persons in high governmental office, diplomats, and members of powerful bureaucracies could seal the fate of others. They could choose. They could either do their job and submit to the orders of their government, or they could disobey the mandates of their superiors. Embassies and consulates throughout the Nazi era were filled with hundreds of officials in high places who could choose to find refuge for those made homeless, or bow to the orders of extermination instead. The choice of conscience demands a high

There is a serious price to be paid for the exercise of conscience.

price. Few officials were willing to defy the order of their bureaucratic superiors, knowing that defiance of authority meant dismissal, disgrace, and worse for themselves and their families. A visa or passport carried the stamp of destiny, a blessing for the stateless, but a curse for those who violated diplomatic protocol.

Mordechai Paldiel, the longtime director of the Righteous Among the Nations department at Yad Vashem, wrote a small but profoundly significant book based on documented records of twenty-nine diplomats who acted in a heroic fashion during the sinister years of the Holocaust.[9] These diplomats of conscience made valiant decisions while fully cognizant of the punishments they would receive and the poverty and humiliation they would endure were they to disobey orders from above. For these government representatives who had pledged allegiance to the protocols of obedience, saving lives was treasonable. Their courageous duty to disobey provides the civilized denizens of the world with a resounding truth: there was and always is an alternative to complicity with tyranny.

Among a small minority of diplomats, many suffered consequences for their altruism. These diplomats of irrepressible conscience came from many different lands: China, Spain, Portugal, Romania, Switzerland, Brazil, Holland, Turkey, Italy, the Vatican, Yugoslavia, Japan, and Germany. Life and death were in their hands. They chose life. They issued exit and entrance visas, letters of protection, and passports giving new protected status to Jews made homeless. They issued false stamps, invented new documents to impress the border guards, cajoled, bluffed, lied, and threatened authorities to save stranded Jews unprotected from harsh laws and hooligan informers. For loosening the fetters of the chained, they received severe punishments from the superiors of their respective governments.

Who can enter the minds and souls of these heroic diplomats, who knew that their acts might forfeit their coveted status, abolish their protected pensions, and impoverish their families? Where do such acts of altruism figure into the sad portrayal of human nature? Are their acts done for power, sex, or fame, or are they rather awesome reminders of the goodness in human nature?

Aristides de Sousa Mendes: Undiplomatic Diplomacy

From 1938 to 1940, Aristides de Sousa Mendes, a Portuguese consul general stationed in Bordeaux, France, faced pitiable crowds of refugees from the German invasion of France, camped in the streets and parks before his embassy, all desperately seeking visas to allow them exit to Spain and Portugal. Unlike others, he refused to shut the blinds of his embassy. He had already received an absolute prohibition against issuing transit visas to refugees, especially to Jews, by Portugal's dictator Antonio de Oliveira Salazar. But Mendes could not bear standing idly by the fateful choice of the blessing and curse set before him. After agonizing for days and nights, he cut himself off from the world and announced to his staff, "I'm giving everyone visas. There will be no more nationalities, races, or religions."[10] With the German army fast approaching Bordeaux, Mendes spent the whole day signing visas and asked no questions. Rabbi Haim Kruger, one of the refugees stranded in Bordeaux, pleaded for his abandoned Jewish community, sitting by Mendes for a full day without food and sleep and helping him stamp thousands of passports with Portuguese visas.

Mendes, age fifty-five and the father of twelve children, was repeatedly implored by his staff, for the sake of his wife and children and his own safety, to stop his violations of government edicts. To his staff, Mendes spoke these words:

> My government has denied all applications for visas to any refugees, but I cannot allow these people to die. Many are Jews, and our constitution says that the religion, or politics, of a foreigner shall not be used to deny him refuge in Portugal. I have decided to follow this principle. I am going to issue a visa to anyone who asks for it, regardless of whether or not he can pay … even if I am dismissed, I can only act as a Christian, as my conscience tells me.[11]

Mendes hoped that his wife and children would understand the risk that he was taking, but he remained confident that what he was doing was just and righteous. He wrote:

> I know that Mrs. Mendes wholly concurs with my views, and I feel certain that my children will understand and not hold it against me if by giving out a visa to each and everyone of the refugees, I am tomorrow discharged from my duties for having acted contrarily to orders, which in my estimation are vile and unjust. And so I declare that I shall give, free of charge, a visa to whomsoever shall request it. My desire is to be with God against man, rather than with man against God.[12]

No matter the authority of the mandate, orders incompatible with human compassion should not be obeyed. Repeatedly chastised by other ambassadors for giving shelter "to the scum of democratic regimes," Mendes responded, "Why don't you help

those poor refugees? How would you like to find yourself, your
wife and children, in the same circumstances as the refugees?"
Mendes added:

> It is obvious that the attitude I took could not fail to
> cause strangeness. However, it should be noted that
> everything was strange at the time. My attitude was in
> fact the result of the totally abnormal circumstances
> of force majeure ... It must be that I made mistakes.
> But if I did so, it was not on purpose. For I've always
> acted according to my conscience. I was guided solely
> by a sense of duty, fully aware of my responsibilities.[13]

Those who accused Mendes of disloyalty, such as Francisco
Calheiros e Meneses, the Portuguese ambassador in Brussels, dismissed the imperatives of conscience as egregious. As Mendes
wrote, "The witness is well aware that a functionary has no need
to be humane when it is a question of obeying orders, whatever
they may be."[14] For Meneses, the only plausible explanation for
Mendes's actions was that the poor man must have been overcome by a strange moral sentiment. At his trial, the Portuguese
authorities recommended suspension of Mendes's duties and
pay. For his premeditated disobedience, he was demoted to the
rank below that of consul. Salazar, however, overruled that punishment and insisted that Mendes be dismissed from active
service for one year, and on half-pay, and thereafter be forced to
retire. Bereft of any income, with a family of twelve children to
feed, Mendes was forced to sell his estate in Cabanas de Veriato.
The Jewish community in Lisbon granted Mendes a monthly
allowance. The Mendes family ate at the Jewish soup kitchen.

There is a serious price to be paid for the exercise of conscience. Diplomats like Mendes often forfeited position, posses-
sions, and prestige to follow their conscience. Mendes is one of
the Christian rescuers whose life deserves to be honored and
studied by theologians, ethicists, and social scientists. Goodness
must be searched, understood, and taught. Each year brings

new testimony of the capacity of human beings to hurt and to heal. Both capacities reside within human nature, and both potentialities can be actualized; both offer a fuller anthropology.

The search and discovery of altruistic behavior speaks of a critical connection between divine and human nature. The testimony of the rescuers and the rescued calls upon philosophers, theologians, and social scientists to evaluate the implications of the culture of altruistic disobedience within systems of conformity. The religious tradition in Judaism calls for *hakarat hatov*, the recognition of goodness.

Sempo Sugihara

Sempo Sugihara, the Japanese consul general in Kuanas, Lithuania, understood his government's orders after Lithuania was overrun and annexed by the Soviet Union as part of the Ribbentrop-Molotov pact. Jews were caught between Nazi and Soviet persecution. Many had escaped from Poland and sought to get out of Lithuania. Their only escape was to flee eastward. They begged for Japanese transit visas to get them to other countries via Japan. Large crowds of pleading Jews with tears in their eyes desperately sought visas to live. The diplomat was duty-bound to obey the orders of his superiors but plagued by the plight of mothers and children with expressions of terror and hunger. Conscience triumphed over duty, courage and compassion overruled protocol. Sempo Sugihara issued 3,500 transfer visas to Jews. His government superiors were infuriated and he was repeatedly chastised. Nonetheless, Sugihara's conscience was irrepressible, as he declared firmly, "I will not pay any attention to these strictures. I act solely out of love for people and humanitarian feeling."[15]

> The search and discovery of altruistic behavior speaks of a critical connection between divine and human nature.

Returning home, Sugihara was summoned by the foreign ministry of Tokyo and asked to resign. He and his family suffered dishonor and humiliation from his government.

Shortly before his death in 1986, Sugihara was asked about his motives. He had this to say:

> You want to know about my motivations, don't you? Well, it is the kind of sentiments anyone would have when he actually sees the refugees face-to-face, begging with tears in their eyes. He just cannot help but sympathize with them. Among the refugees were the elderly and women. They were so desperate that they went so far as to kiss my shoes. Yes. I actually witnessed such things with my own eyes ... People in Tokyo were not unified [on a proper refugee policy]. I felt it kind of silly to deal with them. So I made up my mind not to wait for their reply. I knew that somebody would surely complain to me in the future. But I myself thought this would be the right thing to do. There is nothing wrong in saving many people's lives. If anybody sees anything wrong in the action, it is because "not pure" exists in their state of mind. The spirit of humanity, philanthropy, neighborly friendship ... with this spirit, I ventured to do what I did, confronting this most difficult situation—and because of this reason, I went ahead with redoubled courage.[16]

Mordechai Paldiel noted ironically that diplomats like Sugihara faced two choices: to do the right thing for the wrong reason or to do the wrong thing for the right reason. There is obedience that betrays God and disobedience that magnifies God's presence and goodness. As we read in Deuteronomy: "I have set before you this day of life and prosperity, death and adversity ... I have put before you life and death—blessing and curse. Choose life—if you and your offspring would live" (30:15, 19).

Conversation with a German Pastor

In April 1962, I was invited to Germany to interview Christian clergy who, resisting the Nazis, had disobeyed the pronouncements of both church and state. I made contact with Pastor Henrich Gruber of Berlin-Klausendorf. During the Holocaust, Gruber had established an underground bureau that spirited hundreds of Jews out of Nazi Germany. Gruber, repeatedly warned by the Nazis to keep his tongue, continued to preach against the Nazis, was thrown into jail, and was sent to Sachsenhausen concentration camp, where all his teeth were knocked out by the Nazi guards. (During our conversation, Gruber would occasionally smile and point to his false teeth.) Gruber refused to stop denouncing the persecution of Jews and continued to rescue as many Jews as he could. For this defiance, he was sent to Dachau.

During our private conversation in May 1962, Gruber railed against the servile silence of the churches during the Holocaust. I asked him what good it would have done if the clergy had spoken out against the government. His words impacted my memory as he sighed his response:

> Rabbi, if a hundred German priests and pastors had put on their clerical collars and church vestments and marched in the streets in the city squares of Berlin in protest against the barbaric treatment of your people, the fate of your people would be altogether different, and so would our conversation.

I persisted. Did Gruber really believe that street protests could have made any difference? He answered:

> The Nazis started a program of euthanasia to systematically wipe out the weak of body and mind. They exterminated 250,000 Germans whom they called the "*Lebensunwertes*," those unfit for life: the sick, maimed, crippled, disabled. In August 1942,

> Hitler's order came to a swift halt. It was no miracle. Germans, ordinary Germans, marched in protest before the Nazi quarters, and priests like Bishop Wurm of the Lutheran Church and Father Bernhard Lichtenberg protested the sinister plan of the Nazis. Euthanasia was stopped in its tracks ... When German Christian women married to Jews saw that their husbands were imprisoned and jailed and would end up in concentration camps, hundreds of their wives marched in the streets before the Gestapo headquarters on *Rosenstraasse*, and in March 1943, the Nazis released [them].

Witnesses to goodness help teach us that there are acts of obedience that are blasphemous and acts of disobedience that are sacred. Months later, after my meeting with Pastor Gruber, I came across a Talmudic passage (Avodah Zarah 18b). In that section of the Talmud, the Rabbis debated whether Jews should attend the Roman arena where gladiators were pitted against wild beasts and against each other while the spectator mob would decide the fate of the victim. The Roman procurator would signal to the mob; should he point his thumb downward, the victim's fate was sealed.

> Witnesses to goodness help teach us that there are acts of obedience that are blasphemous and acts of disobedience that are sacred.

Appalled by such vicious sport, the Rabbis ruled that the Roman arena was a vile and horrific place and that Jews were prohibited from entering it. Rabbi Nathan demurred. To the contrary, he ruled, "Let Jews attend the arena, so that when the bloodletting mob stands on its feet and cries 'Thumbs down!' let the Jews rise up as one and cry out, 'Thumbs up!'" Not to go to the stadium would only evade the grimness of reality. To attend the stadium and remain silent would allow the frenzied mob to prevail. The sages ruled to let those who attend scream and point their thumbs upward. As a commentator explains, perhaps the beasts will be frightened by the screams and the heart of the procurator may melt. Whoever does not protest against evil collaborates with evil. This is the sacred duty to disobey.

6

The Conscience of an Anti-Semite

Heaven does not grant halves.
—Talmud, Sanhedrin 64a

With his bare hands, Samson tore asunder a full-grown lion. He looked at the remains of the lion's skeleton and found a swarm of bees and honey. "He scooped it into his hands and ate it as he went along." Later, Samson propounded a riddle to his thirty companions and promised a reward for anyone who could offer the right answer: "Out of the eater came something to eat. Out of the strong came something sweet" (Judg. 14:14).

Can sweetness come out of the jaws of bitterness? Can carnivorous evil give birth to life-saving acts of altruism? In her book *When Light Pierced the Darkness*, sociologist Nechama Tec includes accounts of her interviews with people who were—and some who remained—vile anti-Semites during and after the Holocaust. Paradoxically, some of them have their names inscribed as Righteous Gentiles in Israel's Holocaust center, Yad Vashem. Out of the toxic bitterness of virulent anti-Semitism, there emerged an unanticipated sweetness from those anti-Semitic rescuers who saved those whom they held in contempt.

The Enigma of Anti-Semitic Rescuers

Hela Horska was a nurse married to a prominent Polish physician. They were both devout Catholics and members of the Nationalist Democratic Movement, an organization noted for its overt anti-Semitism. The Horskas were surrounded by a circle of obsessive anti-Semites who accused Jews of disloyalty, economic exploitation, and intrinsic foreignness. The miasma of anti-Semitism hung in the air. Jews were barred from employment in state-owned industries, and Jewish businesses were to be boycotted. Hela Horska had no love for Jews before or after World War II. Jews, she told her friends, deliberately spread lies of Polish anti-Semitism to convince other Jews to go to Israel and serve in the Israeli army. After the war, Hela's son was offered the opportunity to study cancer research medicine in Israel. When he developed a low white blood cell count and died, Hela Horska said, "If Jews had given him work in another field, he would have been alive today." Despite her persistent anti-Semitism, Hela Horska turned her home into a transit system to hide and save Jews during the Holocaust years, saving fourteen Jews from death, keeping a Jewish family in her home, and seeing to it that other Poles hid those pursued by the predators.

> Good is not evil and evil is not good, but to our amazement, out of evil goodness may spring.

Helping Jews in Poland by taking them in for a night or giving them a lift in a vehicle of any sort was a capital crime. As early as October 15, 1941, Governor General Hans Frank published an ordinance stating unambiguously that persons who deliberately offered a hiding place to Jews would be subject to the same punishment meted out to the Jews they protected. The Polish rescuers feared not only the Nazi predators but also the Polish *Schmaltzonikis*, or extortionists, who would inform the

Gestapo about the hiders and the hidden for a bottle of whiskey or a pack of cigarettes.

Nechama Tec interviewed Hela Horska and David Rodman, one of the fourteen Jews she hid. Rodman recalled a deeply religious retired railroad worker and farmer named Lech Sarna, who agreed to hide Horska's Jews in his barn. Later, Sarna grew deeply conflicted, particularly after attending church. He declared that he was frightened for his soul lest he forfeit the rewards of heaven for helping Jews. Regretting his decision to shelter Jews, he asked Hela Horska to take them back. Hela responded by calling in her children as if to shame him, and she spoke these caustic words before Lech Sarna: "You go to church and commune with God and you are willing to deprive my children of their life?" Lech relented and continued to protect the Jews.

What accounts for such anomalous behavior? The motivation was not money, sexual favor, or fame. Quite the contrary. A Jewish man, learning that the Horskas were hiding Jews, pleaded for shelter and promised them $25,000 if they would hide him and his wife. Hela was indignant:

> Sir, do you think for $100,000 dollars I would lend you my children? If I do help Jews, I want to. And if I can, I will do it without money. It is almost insulting. My children are dear to me. You know that I can lose them, so it is not a matter of money here. It is a question of what I can do.

Such cases of anti-Semitic rescuers are rare, but for that all the more arresting. Interviewing a Jewish survivor, Vera Elman, Nechama Tec records the activity of a devout Catholic woman name Kormonica, who was unmarried, disfigured, and filled with venomous anti-Semitic sentiments. Kormonica held contempt for Jews and yet risked her life to save them. She told Vera Elman, "You know how religious I am, but if Christ would stand before me and Hitler, through Christ's body I would knife him down." When Kormonica grew ill, Vera Elman cared for her. Kormonica died in Vera's arms.

Eva Fleischner, a researcher who investigated French behavior toward the Jews during the Nazi occupation, interviewed a Protestant pastor whose cultural hero was the vicious anti-Semite Charles Mauras. Asked about his attitude toward Jews and whether he would shelter them, the minister answered, "I can't stand Jews, but if you bring me a Jew, I'll give my life for him."

Zophia and Zegota

Zofia Kossak-Szczucka, a woman from a socially prominent Polish family, a devout Catholic, and a member of the nationalist, rightist, and rabidly anti-Semitic Catholic organization FOP, was instrumental in creating the Zegota, the council for aid to Jews during the Holocaust years. The Zegota is credited for saving between 40,000 and 50,000 Jewish adults and 2,500 Jewish children. The Zegota hid Jews, offered them medical assistance, forged certificates, and paid off money to blackmailers. Zofia sounded the first public demand to establish such an underground organization to save Jews. She published a leaflet called "The Protest" in 1942, addressed to the Polish people, that described the hellish conditions in the Warsaw Ghetto, where executioners ran wild through the streets, shooting anyone who dared leave his or her house. The leaflet described streets full of unburied corpses, with the number of victims of the Nazis ranging from 8,000 to 10,000 daily:

> The world looks upon this murder as more horrible than anything that history has ever seen and they are silent. The slaughter of millions of defenseless people is carried out in a general sinister silence ... Silent are Poles. This silence can no longer be tolerated. Whatever the reason for it, it is vile. In the face

of murder it is wrong to remain passive. Whoever is silent witnessing murder becomes a partner to the murder. Whoever does not condemn, consents. Therefore we Catholics, Poles, raise our voices.[1]

"The Protest" contained an incongruous mixture of profound empathy for Jews and unrelenting anti-Semitism. As she wrote:

Our feelings toward the Jews have not changed. We continue to deem them political, economic and ideological enemies of Poland. Moreover, we realize that they hate us more than they hate the Germans, and that they make us responsible for their misfortune. Why, and on what basis, remains a mystery of the Jewish soul. Nevertheless, this is a decided fact.[2]

Zofia's protest continued with a powerful condemnation of Catholics and Poles who looked on as Jewish children who could not walk on their own strength were brutally loaded onto wagons headed toward torture and annihilation. Zofia writes: "The executioners pack the condemned into the wagons and later railcar death cars, one-hundred-and-fifty of them in one railcar. On the floor lies a thick layer of lime and chlorine, poured over with water."[3] She described the sealing of the doors, the people crammed tightly so that "the dead cannot fall and keep standing arm-in-arm with the living." Where and whenever the death wagons will arrive, Zofia noted, they will only contain corpses.

It is confounding to live with the ambivalence of human nature, yet to live aware of human ambiguity is to recognize the complexity and potentialities in living.

Addressing her Polish coreligionists, Zofia acknowledged that they can neither help nor rescue anybody. "But we protest from the bottom of our hearts filled with pity, indignation and horror. This protest is demanded of us by God, who does not allow us to kill. It is demanded by our Christian conscience."[4] While her anti-Semitism leaks through even in her protest of the persecution of the Jews, Zofia somehow managed to transcend her deep-seated prejudice. She called for an underground organization to save Jews and by the end of 1942, the Zegota was born. In 1943, Zofia was caught and sent to Auschwitz. After her release nearly a year later, she resumed her work, becoming especially active in the rescue of Jewish children by hiding them in convents and other institutions run by the clergy.

Good is not evil and evil is not good, but to our amazement, out of evil goodness may spring.

Motivations for Altruism

How are we to understand the oxymoronic phrase "anti-Semitic rescuers of Jews"? What motivations may be ascribed to the gentile rescuers of Jews? We are faced with the mystique of goodness. The unpredictability of the self-sacrificing behavior of gentile rescuers befuddles the researchers. A variety of theories have been proposed to account for altruistic behavior. I recall a private conversation with my friend, psychologist Perry London, who speculated that rescuers shared a background of marginality and adventuresomeness that placed them outside conventional behavior. Other researchers explained their altruism as a consequence of parental influence. Still others suggested that altruistic behavior may be traced to a religious upbringing. And then there were rescuers whose parents were antireligious and anti-Semitic Nazi sympathizers but who revolted against the meanness of their parents' outlook and turned proactively philo-Semitic.

The search for altruistic motivation is full of anomalies, filled with "and yet," "nevertheless," and "in spite of" surprises. For some churchgoers, Jews were to be saved because Christ was a Jew; for others, Jews were not to be saved because Christ was crucified by Jews. Theories of motivation abound, no sooner proposed than contradicted. Some researchers maintain that the strong bond to community accounts for the rescuers' sense of responsibility; yet other rescuers can claim no such upbringing. Some rescuers reported having Jewish friends, but just as many reported not having any. Many rescuers are said to have had high self-esteem and were therefore more prone to active intervention, yet many more people with high self-esteem remained indifferent bystanders.

Undoubtedly, the motivations for altruism are varied, but what the rescuers shared in common was a moral conscience that emboldened them to disobey evil authorities. Their moral sensibility may have come from different sources of belonging, behaving, and believing—parents, churches, teachers, and friends—but whatever their origin, they held in common a deep conviction as to what was right and what was wrong. Conscience enabled them to transcend their upbringing, circumstances, and associations. Anti-Semitic rescuers were able to overcome the prejudices of their family, church, and friends. Moral conscience bridles at the reins of conformity that harness people to secular or religious authoritarian institutions.

The Ambiguity of Good and Evil

The paradoxical stories of anti-Semitic rescuers of Jews calls to mind elements of the Jewish mystic tradition that wrestle with the ambivalent mystique of goodness and evil. A rabbinic midrash avers that whether or not an infant will grow up healthy or sick, strong or weak, rich or poor, may be determined by God, but the possession of character remains a mystery.

The mystique of good and evil is prefigured in a nightmare that haunted the Baal Shem Tov, the eighteenth-century "Master of the Good Name." In his dream, a dark heart incarnated with the demonic forces of evil appeared to him. The Baal Shem Tov was frightened, then enraged, and finally he resolved to destroy the evil heart. He clenched his fist and pounded furiously against the cruel heart, intending to rid the world of all the sinister powers within it. In the midst of his frenzy, the Baal Shem Tov stopped. From within the dark heart, he heard the sobbing of an infant and wondered how such innocence could exist within the cauldron of hellish evil.

The dream and its interpretations may stem from a Kabbalistic insight in the Zohar:

> When God came to create the world and reveal what was hidden in the depths and disclose light out of darkness, they were all wrapped in one another, and therefore light emerged from darkness and from the impenetrable came the profound, so too, from good issues evil and from mercy issues judgment, and all are intertwined, the good impulse and the evil impulse, right and left, Israel and other peoples, white and black—all depend upon one another. (380b and 63ab)

Capturing the Evil Tempter

How can we account for altruism toward Jews in the heart of anti-Semitic enemies? We tend to see our heroes and villains neatly labeled as either good or bad, saintly or demonic. Such split thinking polarizes people and renders simplistic judgments. It is confounding to live with the ambivalence of human nature, yet to live aware of human ambiguity is to recognize the complexity and potentialities in living.

In a remarkable passage in the Talmud (Sanhedrin 64a), the interdependence of good and evil is dramatized. When the cries of a fiery lion's whelp came forth from the Holy of Holies, the prophet identified it as "the tempter of idolatry, the essence of evil." The sages pondered what to do with the malevolent tempter. They first prayed that the tempter of sin be delivered into their hands. The prayer was granted and the sages imprisoned temptation for three days. But days after the incarceration of temptation, no newly laid egg in the whole of Palestine was to be found. They came to understand that without temptation, sex, family, or civilization cannot prevail.

The sages wondered, "What shall we do? Shall we pray that this power be partially destroyed? Shall we pray that only the lust and impulses that promote good should remain alive, while those that are for evil should be destroyed? Let lust be restricted to matrimonial sexuality alone but be abolished for extramarital relationships? Let anger be released for righteous indignation against injustice, but otherwise let anger be extinguished?" The sages' pleading was met with a profound response: "Heaven does not grant halves" (*palga barakia lo yehavei*) (B. Yoma 69b). The world is not created with hermetically sealed packages marked "Good" and "Evil." Good and evil are intertwined and both are found within one parcel. Sparks of goodness may be discovered in the ashes of crematoria, and in the Holy of Holies an evil tempter may be hidden. Moral conscience resides in odd places, in unlikely persons, and in strange times. It requires a discerning wisdom to observe the blending of virtue and vice in life. "Heaven does not grant halves."

Conventionally, we would have our adversaries demonized and our heroes flawless. Martin Gilbert, the distinguished historian, recounts that when Oscar Schindler, the celebrated rescuer of Jews, was chosen in 1961 to be honored by planting a tree in the Avenue of the Righteous, the protests against his selection were so great that Schindler was unable to leave his hotel in order to plant a tree. He was compelled to wait there for three days until he could be taken unannounced to Yad Vashem for a private ceremony.[5] Schindler, after all, was a German and a former member of the Nazi party. Was such a tarnished man to be honored? When in 1968 a leading Hollywood film company approached Yad Vashem to make a film about Schindler's rescue, they asked the museum to put them in touch with some of the survivors of Schindler's rescue efforts. They were refused on the grounds that it would be unsuitable for a German to be portrayed as the first of rescuers and be given film recognition. How can conscience be acknowledged to reside in the soul of a former Nazi party member, a carouser, an adulterer, a womanizer, a wheeler-dealer, a gambler, and a hard drinker? Such is the mystique of the coexistence of good and evil in one vessel.

Ecclesiastes contends that there "is no person who does good and does not sin" (7:20), to which we may add that there are those who sin and do good. Nothing exists unalloyed. Good and evil cohabit. "Better," Ecclesiastes counsels, to "grasp the one without letting go of the other" (7:18).

From the wisdom of holistic vision we can decipher an answer to Samson's riddle: "Out of the eater came something to eat. Out of the strong came something sweet." Conscience is a mystery that may lodge in the strangest of venues and emerge in the oddest of persons, and in the most bizarre of times.

7

CULTIVATING CONSCIENCE

One pang of conscience is worth more than many lashes.
—YOSSI B. HALAFTA, B. BERACHOTH 7A

Obedience and Authority

Totalitarian regimes like Nazism, fascism, and communism are not alone. Democracies as well have succumbed to the dominant culture of soulless obedience. The history of the freest country in the world records the dark stains of a people still traumatized by the torment and humiliation of enslavement. The United States' culture of mindless obedience allowed slavery, condoned the exploitation of Native Americans, complied with the humiliating internment of thousands of Japanese-Americans, abandoned poor African Americans flailing in the toxic waters of Hurricane Katrina, and feigned deafness, blindness, and muteness before the disgrace at Guantanamo and Abu Ghraib. In the name of mob obedience, conscience is crushed, and in its place an endlessly reiterated Nuremberg rationale is proffered to justify mass murder. At the Nuremberg trials, Nazi judges, lawyers, doctors, and clergy hid behind the same justifications for their callous, sadistic behavior: obedience, law, and order. Millions of people were systematically murdered on command. Hitler, they reminded us, was elected as the Fuehrer, and every one of his dictates was legally and dutifully followed.

Obedience to obedience was a habit of culture that smothered the critical sensibility of conscience. "Commandedness"— *obrigkeit, gehorsam, pficht*—dampened the spark of moral resistance. Good citizens, good churchgoers, good soldiers, and good industrialists obey their superiors. Good people goose-step in the genocidal parade responsive to the barks of the commanders. Obedience to obedience justifies any action and belief, while moral disobedience is labeled treason, sabotage, and heresy.

Rudolf Hess, the commandant of Auschwitz, the largest and most notorious of the Nazi concentration camps in Poland, wrote a memoir titled *Fuehrer, You Order. We Obey,* in which he states that he himself "never hated Jews." When Heinrich Himmler personally gave him orders in December 1941 to prepare a place for mass killings and to carry out those assignments, Hess claimed never to have imagined the scale of this monstrous design. Still, Hess never hesitated:

> I have received an order; I have to carry it out. I could not allow myself to form an opinion as to whether this order for extermination of the Jews was necessary or not. At the time it was beyond my frame of mind. Since the Fuehrer himself had ordered "The Final Solution" to the "Jewish Question," there was no second questioning for an old national socialist, much less an S.S. Officer.[1]

Hess confessed that he was sickened by the bloodbaths, and that there were suicides among the rank of Special S.S. Death Squads who could no longer mentally endure wading in the bloodbaths. But Hess added:

> Outsiders cannot possibly understand that there was not a single S.S. Officer who would refuse to

obey orders from Himmler because of the severely harsh orders. Whatever the Fuehrer or Himmler ordered was always right. Even democratic England has a saying, "My Country, Right or Wrong," and every patriotic Englishman follows it.[2]

So exalted was the culture of obedience that suicide was deemed preferable to disobedience. At the Nuremburg Trials, the Reichmarshall and Luftwaffe Chief Hermann Goering cynically observed that people don't want war, but that "it is the leaders of the country who determine the policy and it is always a simple matter to drag the people along, whether it is a democracy or a fascist dictatorship or a communist dictatorship."[3]

Goering's chilling insight contains a terrifying truth. The overbearing dominance of the culture of obeisance was and remains a universal danger to conscience. Democracies are not exempt. Was what happened during the Holocaust so extraordinary that such cruelty could take place only in the fog of war, and only in the sinister shadows of totalitarianism? Could cruelty happen under the banner of peace and beneath the flag of democracy?

Abu Ghraib and the "Prison" of Stanford

By May 2004, the shocking pictures of Abu Ghraib in Iraq had become well known throughout the world: naked men stacked high in a pyramid; American soldiers grinning as a female soldier leads around a nude captive by a dog leash tied around his neck; prisoners ordered to masturbate and to simulate fellatio in front of a cigarette-smoking female soldier; prisoners forced to cover their heads with women's pink panties; and guards using unmuzzled attack dogs to frighten the prisoners.

For Philip G. Zimbardo, a leading social psychologist at Stanford University, the sadistic behavior of American soldiers at Abu Ghraib prison came as no surprise. Zimbardo claimed to

have seen, much earlier, parallel pictures of prisoners with bags
on their heads and sadistic behavior by civilian students, all
detailed in his experiment at Stanford University. In *The Lucifer
Effect*, Zimbardo and his researchers report the events at a simu-
lated prison in a Stanford

> Obedience to
> obedience was a habit
> of culture that
> smothered the critical
> sensibility of
> conscience.

University basement in August
1971.[4] Twenty-four undergraduate
students were recruited to play
prison guards and prisoners for
two weeks. The students were typi-
cal healthy, intelligent, college students. In less than a week, many of
the "guards" had, of their own
accord, become swaggering and
sadistic wardens, placing bags over the prisoners heads, "forcing
them to strip naked and encouraging them to perform sexual
acts." At one point, the guards in the feigned prison ordered one
group of anxious and disturbed prisoners to strip and assume the
role of female camels, bent over, while another group was told,
"You are the male camels," ordering them to simulate sex.

Professor Zimbardo and his colleagues were so shocked by
the intensity of the "guards'" domination and the obedience of
the student "prisoners" that they voluntarily ended the experiment more than a week earlier than initially planned. The students assigned to play guards were not instructed to be abusive,
but conformed to their own ideas on how to keep order. Prisoners
were blindfolded, stripped, assigned numbers, and forced to wear
ankle chains. The guards were given handcuffs and billy clubs; the
majority of them conformed, complied, and obeyed.

How can students, born and bred in an American democracy, do such horrendous things under orders, and even pose for
such pictures? Where were the guards who could cry out "No!" to
such cruel and humiliating behavior? Where was conscience?

Excuses for this kind of outrageous behavior at Stanford
were much the same as those used to account later for the

obscene conduct at Abu Ghraib. This torturous conduct, it was claimed, was the work of "rogue guards," a few "bad apples" thrown in the barrel.

Zimbardo repudiates such self-serving exculpatory explanations. How comfortable to believe that there were but a few rotten apples at the bottom of a barrel to blame for their madness. Better to focus on the barrel itself, its rottenness, and the contaminating culture of complicity with authority figures. Zimbardo argues that disproportionate attention has been given to the individual character faults of perpetrators to account for their compliance, while the corrupting environment and the situations encouraged by the system of conformity is overlooked.

I am convinced that courage, bravery, heroism, altruism, and acts of conscience ought not be simplistically traced to private and personal benevolent dispositions. Conscienceless cruelty, disloyalty, and denigration of others cannot be accounted for by reference to inborn malevolent dispositions. The moral heroism, as well as the sadism of the predators cited in the previous chapters, did not stem from occult, innate benevolent or deviant proclivities. The rotten barrel more than the rotten apples requires scrutiny. An immoral barrel creates an ambience of subservience to authorities, whether they are wearing the white coats of social science experiments or black, red, or brown uniforms.

War stories as well as sociological experiments reveal the conforming environment that conditions our behavior. In a 2007 report for the *Los Angeles Times*, the accounts of distinguished reporter Chris Hedges reveal the culture of contempt among the U.S. forces in Iraq. With extraordinary honesty, U.S. veterans, medics, MPs, artillerymen, snipers, and officers report the indiscriminate killings of civilians carried out by American soldiers. Home raids on "cordon and search" operations were carried out with ruthless abandon; homes were turned upside down and family patriarchs humiliated in front of their children. Many members of the soldiers' units viewed the Iraqis as

little better than *Hajji*, an Arabic terms for those who make the
Hajj pilgrimage. "*Hajji* food" and "*hajji* homes" became slurs.

Hedges points to a survey released in May 2007 by the
Pentagon that indicated that only 47 percent of the soldiers and
38 percent of the Marines agreed that civilians should be treated
with dignity and respect, and that only 55 percent of soldiers
and 40 percent of Marines said they would report a unit member who had killed or injured "an innocent non-combatant."
Furthermore, veterans had little good to say about senior military officers who encouraged reckless behavior, though they
themselves spent most of their time in heavily fortified com-
pounds and rarely saw combat. The rotten barrel represents the
unmitigated culture of obedience that indoctrinates the denigration and dehumanization of prisoners and guards alike.

The Milgram Experiment

Professor Stanley Milgram of Yale University writes: "The essence
of obedience consists in the fact that a person comes to view
himself as the instrument for carrying out another person's
wishes, and he therefore no longer regards himself as responsible for his actions."[5]

In 1961 Milgram designed "electroshock" experiments to
study the behavior of individuals who voluntarily follow the
orders of others. He was seeking an answer to the pertinent
question: "Could it be that Eichmann and his million accomplices in the Holocaust were just following orders? Could we call
them all accomplices?"[6]

Milgram divided the subjects of his experiment into "teachers" and "learners." The teachers were instructed by researchers
dressed in gray laboratory coats to deliver electrical shocks to
learners who gave incorrect answers to some questions.
Unbeknownst to the students in the role of teachers, the learners were instructed to fake their responses as victims and act as
though the fake shocks were painfully real. The teachers

believed that these learners were in fact receiving electric shocks, from 15 to 450 volts. The fake learners, playing their role as instructed, moaned and screamed as the shocks grew in intensity. For the teachers, who knew nothing of this subterfuge, the screams were real and horrifying, and yet most of the them dutifully carried out the instructions of the researcher. A stunning 65 percent of the teachers obeyed the commands all the way to the last potentially lethal switch marked "XXX."

When asked beforehand how many of the teachers they thought would continue to shock the learners when they believed they were inflicting real pain, the psychiatrists in the group guessed perhaps one in a thousand. They were sadly wrong. Almost two-thirds of the teachers continued to shock the learners from 15 to 450 volts, despite the increasing cries and pleas of the victims. Only a small percentage of the teachers stopped and dared defy the orders of the men in gray laboratory coats.

Religion is morally obligated to instill in its adherents the sanctity of conscience that may balance the culture of obedience with the culture of moral disobedience.

Later, when the teachers were asked who was to blame for their outrageous behavior, they answered that the one who gave the orders was to be held responsible, taking no responsibility themselves. The blame was shifted upwards. Those who did stop administering the shocks, on the other hand, did so because they felt responsible for their own actions. They felt that their refusal to obey was a positive, affirmative act following an inner imperative. They understood their disobedience of the external authority as obedience to their own conscience.

The evil confronting civilization in our time cannot be blamed on the few "rotten apples." This past century alone, more than 50 million people were systematically murdered by tens of thousands of unquestioning followers of orders from above. Soldiers and civilians alike lacked the resources of moral disobedience to resist the ethos of "commandedness."

Summarizing one of the fundamental lessons of his experiments, Milgram writes:

> Ordinary people, simply doing their jobs, and without any particular hostility on their part, can become agents in a terrible destructive process. Moreover, even when the destructive effects of their work becomes patently clear, and they are asked to carry out actions incompatible with fundamental standards of morality, relatively few people have the resources needed to resist authority.[7]

Surveying history, the Protestant theologian Reinhold Niebuhr concluded that groups are more immoral than individuals. The urgent challenge for religion is to provide religious groups with the resources needed to resist immoral authority. Religion is morally obligated to instill in its adherents the sanctity of conscience that may balance the culture of obedience with the culture of moral disobedience. It is in the vital interest of religion itself to establish a moral environment in which conscienceless obedience is condemned and moral dissent honored. But the question remains: can religion restrain the groveling at the altar of authoritarian leaders and offer sanctuary to the loyal moral disobedient?

8

THE BRIDGE ACROSS THE RIVERS OF "EITHER-OR"

Things fall apart; the centre cannot hold;
Mere anarchy is loosed upon the world,
The blood-dimmed tide is loosed, and everywhere
The ceremony of innocence is drowned;
The best lack all conviction, while the worst
Are full of passionate intensity.

—WILLIAM BUTLER YEATS,
"THE SECOND COMING"

Who, during such unstable times as ours, can quarrel with the call for heightening obedience to authority? The binding glue of discipline within family, synagogue, state, and business has dried up. Unmoored, we submit to strong personalities and institutions that tell us what to do, when to move, and where to go. Those forces, in turn, feel that only the conforming culture of obedience can hold them together. Yet who among us does not pray for the intervention of dissenting disobedience at critical moments? Who does not hope that somehow, somewhere, someone will walk away from the lever that controls the high voltage torturing the pleading "students" in the Milgram experiment? Who does not anxiously await the angel of conscience to come on time to stand between Abraham's knife and his beloved child, Isaac? Who does not bless the angel who overrides the imperative of God to sacrifice the son and says, "Do not raise your hand against the boy, or do anything to him" (Gen. 22:12)? Is it not to the intervention of the angel of conscience that we owe our lives and the lives of our children?

Knowing what we know about the perfidy following blind obedience to authority, is religion not duty-bound to raise parishioners of conscience to counter the repressive culture of conformity? Does organized religion want to raise citizens of conscience, people who are motivated to protect the persecuted and to oppose regimes that stoke the fires of crematoria? Or does religion fear conscience as a threat to its own authority and wish to subdue it? Is religion, in effect, complicit with the authoritarian societies that strangle the voice of prophetic conscience? Is it willing to welcome conscience into its ecclesiastical bosom?

Either-Or: The Way Options Are Shared

What prevents religion from actively making room in its house for moral and intellectual critique? To a large extent, organized religion is entrapped by its own schismatic "either-or" thinking. It sees the world through the absolutistic choices of hard disjunctives: either obedience or disobedience; either subservience to authority or anarchy; either acceptance or rebellion. Organized religion appears unable to envision the interdependent coexistence of obedience and disobedience, a time to obey and a time to disobey.

No one more ecstatically eulogized "either-or" faith and demonized "both-and" resolution than the nineteenth-century Danish philosopher Søren Kierkegaard, whose personal sobriquet was "Either-Or."

> Either/or is the word at which the folding doors fly
> open and the ideals appear—Oh, blessed sight!

> Either/or is the pass which admits to the absolute,
> God be praised. Yes, either/or is the key to heaven ...
> both/and is the key to hell.[1]

The seductive power of either-or faith lies in its absolute certainty. Stand on one side or the other; no straddling allowed. Yes or no, no qualifications permitted. Beware of the telltale signs of "both-and" synthesis—the weasel words such as "however," "on the other hand," "perhaps," "having said that." These are verbal indices of equivocation, the betrayal of absolute fidelity to a commanding God who will be obeyed unequivocally. With such a conception of unquestioning faith, no argument—rational or moral—will be countenanced. The command is to be obeyed without human evaluation.

The ideal representation of the either-or faith is the figure of biblical Abraham, who hears the unequivocal command: "Take your son, your favored one, Isaac, whom you love and go to the land of Moriah and offer him as a burnt offering on one of the heights that I will point out to you" (Gen. 22:2). Either-or demands but one answer: *"Hineni"*—"Here I am." More than the sacrifice of the son is demanded. The sacrifice of moral conscience is laid on the sacrificial altar. Caught in the vise of either-or, there is no room for a third alternative. Either black or white precludes gray; either yes or no precludes maybe. Either-or dismisses the challenges of conscience as blasphemy. Whether, what, when, and whom to obey raises questions offensive to the Grand Commander.

Through conscience, the voices of heaven and earth are brought together.

Normative Judaism, we have maintained, repudiates such schismatic thinking. In countless illustrations throughout the rabbinic tradition, no text or authority, no command or commander, is impervious to criticism. Everything and everyone is subject to evaluation.

The pronouncements of divine commander and human rulings by priest and prophet, rabbinical and lay, are subjected to critical evaluation. The claims of no person, divine or human, are exempt from moral challenge.

Not in Heaven But on Earth

One of the most cited Talmudic texts that dramatizes the dignity of human dissent and the refusal of heavenly intervention is found in the Talmud (Baba Metzia 59b). Rabbi Eliezer disputes his colleagues over a matter concerning ritual purity. Rabbi Eliezer brings forth every imaginable argument to sustain his ruling. The sages reject them all. Rabbi Eliezer now resorts to miracles to convince them of the correctness of his judgment. Carob trees are uprooted, streams of water flow backward, the walls of a schoolhouse are bent. None of these miraculous feats is accepted by the sages as justification for Rabbi Eliezer's ruling. Rabbi Eliezer appeals to the heavens, whereupon a heavenly voice cries out, "Why do you dispute with Rabbi Eliezar, seeing that in all matters the halacha agrees with him?" At which point Rabbi Joshua protests, "It is not in heaven." He is saying that the Torah has already been given to us at Mount Sinai and henceforth we pay no attention to heavenly voices.

Rabbi Joshua's outcry rebuffs the intrusion of nonhuman decisions from above. What if Rabbi Joshua had held his tongue? What if the sages had repudiated his protestations and submitted to the voice from heaven in the name of obedience? The entire character of Judaism would have been radically altered by that acquiescence. Reason and morality, compassion and conscience would have been chided as disguised arrogant autonomy. Voices from heaven would replace human argumentations from earth. Rulings and values would be determined solely by supernal revelation, and moral conscience would be dismissed as hubristic humanism. "It is not in heaven" implies that reverent humans bring Torah down to earth. The com-

manding voice of heaven is heard through the earthly disputations between rational and moral men and women. The vertical
chasm between the supernatural and the natural is horizontal-
ized. Heaven and earth are desegregated. The divine is manifest
through the earnest debates and judgments of human beings.

As reported in the Talmud, the response of God to this
exchange between Rabbi Eliezer and Rabbi Joshua is striking.
God rejoices in the mature criticism of the Rabbis. God boasts,
"My children have defeated Me, My sons have defeated Me"
(Baba Metzia 59b). Losing, God wins. God's moral lessons have
been successfully internalized by God's disciples. Through conscience, the voices of heaven and earth are brought together.
There is debate but no animus between commandment and
conscience. Human ears on earth hear the voices from heaven
differently. In heaven, the voice is one, unconditional and
unchanging. On earth, interpretations multiply, the Torah text
loses its literalist rigidity, conflicting majority and minority
opinions are both recorded and cherished. The Rabbis read a
validation of disobedience into a verse from Psalms (119:126):
"It is time to act for the Lord, for they have violated Your
teaching." The sages read out of this verse a principle that
there are times when, for God's sake, the law of God may be put
aside (B. Berachoth 54a). The Torah is opened to diverse and at
times contradictory human interpretations.

A reverent pluralism dwells within ethical monotheism. The
Jewish sages in thirteenth-century France explained that when Moses
ascended to receive the Torah at Sinai, he was shown forty-nine
possibilities to prohibit and forty-nine possibilities to permit in
every case. The possibilities of interpretation should be entrusted
to the sages of each generation and the decision should be in
accordance with their resolution (quoted by Ritba, commentary
on B. Erubin, 13b). The voices of reason and morality sound
diverse interpretations. Times change, situations change, reasons
change. The biblical and Talmudic commentator Rashi observes
that "reasons change in the wake of even only small change in the

situation."[2] At times, one reason is valid, and at times another reason is valid, yet both are "the words of the living God" and both are guided by "one shepherd." When the locus changes from the voice in heaven to the voices on earth, the single note from heaven is expanded into a symphony of meanings on earth.[3]

Abraham Isaac Kook: The Art of Reconciliation

Conventional religion worries that critical conscience sows the seeds of heresy. Conscience, it fears, chips away at religious authority and leaves irreligious secularism in its wake. I argue not only that religion and secularism can live in harmony, but also that they need each other. In this, I am instructed by the spiritual wisdom of the first chief rabbi of Palestine, Abraham Isaac Kook, who was also a noted talmudist, mystic, and poet. Many of his rabbinic colleagues spoke of Kook with disdain because of his unconcealed association with "freethinkers" who denied the existence of God and defied the halachic ritual of observance. Such atheists, Kook's Orthodox colleagues argued, are deserving of anathema, not the loving embrace of a spiritual leader. While his colleagues heard in secular Zionist atheism the voice of apostasy, Kook heard in them the "... painful outcry to liberate man from his narrow and alien pit, to raise him from the darkness of focusing on letters and expressions, to the rights of the thought and feeling, finally to place his primacy on the realm of morals."[4] While his adversaries heard in the unobservant a contempt for faith, Kook recognized an effort to "uproot the dross that separates man from the truly divine hope."[5]

> It is not the moral sensibility of faith that the atheist rejects, but the insensitivity to the aching heart.

Religion, Kook asserted, needs the conscience of atheism to mend the tatters of the faith fabric. Kook was wary of the pious who ordered their lives on the basis of a fixed pattern and were distracted from the flaws of their own practices. Entangled in the minutia of ritual habit, such people are led into lives of mediocrity. Properly understood, Kook averred, atheism is a purifying agent, a cry for "pure morality and heroism for higher things."[6] Atheism itself, however, is misdirected. Its arrows are aimed at the wrong targets. It is not the moral sensibility of faith that the atheist rejects, but the insensitivity to the aching heart.

When his religious colleagues wondered aloud whether the Promised Land was to be rebuilt by secular Zionists whom Kook befriended, Kook responded with a parable of his own: The Holy of Holies could be entered on the Day of Atonement (Yom Kippur), and only by the High Priest dressed in sacred vestments. Yet, Kook continued, when the sanctuary was constructed it was built by secular laborers who entered the sacred precinct with muddy boots and ordinary clothes. Analogously, the Jewish state was and is being built by secular Zionists, so-called unbelievers, who sanctify the land with their blood and sweat.

What would Kook say of the role of conscience in religion? Judging from his religious temperament and approach to those outside the camp of believers, I believe he would welcome conscience as the moral common language of a universe of discourse that may be appealed to by religious and secular Jews. He would search out the unitive values that transcend denominational ideologies. What moral kinship is there between faith and atheism, and what contact between the pieties of supernaturalism and naturalism?

Facing God

What does this committed Orthodox person have in common with an equally committed secular freethinker? Certainly not the supernatural character of God, the Bible, providence, or the afterlife. In the matter of faith, on what may they find any common platform for meaningful discourse?

An intriguing metaphor in the Bible suggests the possibilities of human relationships to Jewish faith that may help bridge their theological differences. In the Bible, Moses repeatedly asks God to reveal God's name, that is, the essence and ways of God. In an act of self-revelation, God informs Moses, "You cannot see My face for men may not see Me and live" (Exod. 33:20). Instead, Moses is stationed in a cleft of the rock where God agrees, "You will see My back; but My face you shall not see. Stationed on the rock, I [God] will make all My goodness pass before you" (33:23). This passage teaches that while no one can actually know God, we may know God's "goodness"—the qualities that reveal God's active essential attributes, such as compassion, slowness to anger, graciousness, and kindness. To know the back of God is to know God's godliness. The face of God is invisible, but the back of God's moral predicates may be known retrospectively. To adapt Kierkegaard's aphorism, we may understand God backward but we must live God forward.

Supernaturalist and naturalist, however they differ as to the presence of God's face, find it easier to agree on the verbs and gerunds behind God's back—caring, healing, helping, making peace. Not the nouns of God's face but the predicates of godliness bring closer differing approaches to faith. We know godliness not by observing the face of the ship but by following the trajectory of its wake. We see, as it were, behind God's back.

Although the same prayer book is held in the hands of grandparents and grandchildren, one person might read it by focusing on its nouns while another centers on its verbs. Whether the source of the virtues of conscience is attributed to a supernatural deity or to the collective conscience of a people, both people may come to see that they share a common understanding and appreciation of the predicates of divinity and the obligation to actualize godliness in their lives. Conscience is the moral nexus that allows interpersonal dialogue, and thereby paves the common ground between different ideas of God, the supernatural, and the natural. Conscience promises a common agenda among the diverse faiths of world religions.

In his *Igrot Rayanah*, Rabbi Kook's vision of oneness (*echad*) led him to reach out to other religions: "At a time such as this, we must clarify the common elements of all religions, according to the degree of their development, and not be afraid of the customary disdain and deep hostility that lurks in the soul against everything alien."[7]

The unitive elements of all religions are embedded in the collective conscience of each faith. Moral conscience lies at the depth of earnest interfaith dialogue. Kook averred that in overcoming our parochialism, the brotherly love of Esau and Jacob, Isaac and Ishmael, may turn into compassion beyond borders. Kook's yearning for wholeness propelled him to overcome the narrowness of religions, and to break down the wall that separates God from humanity. Religious parochialism may be transcended by the shared commonality of moral conscience. Conscience provides pathways among the sacred space of distinctive faiths. As Kook wrote, "Expanse divine my soul craves. Confine me not in cages of substance or of spirit."[8]

Rabbi Kook's ecumenical aspirations call to mind the valiant halachic conscience of Rabbi Menachem Ha-Meiri, one of the rabbinic pioneers at the turn of the fourteenth century. Ha-Meiri wrestled with the issues of Jewish and Christian relations and was himself an eye witness to the expulsion of the Jews from France in 1306. Nevertheless, it was Ha-Meiri who revolutionized Jewish-Christian relations by ruling that the segregating laws and customs in Talmudic times do not apply to Christianity or Islam. The Talmud, which prohibited a host of business, social, and religious relationships with gentiles, intended to protect Judaism from the conduct and behavior of the idolatrous pagans of that period. Such segregating laws and customs, Ha-Meiri maintained, are inapplicable to relations of Jews to Christians and Muslims in our time. Christians and Muslims are not pagans. They belong in the category of "nations restricted by the ways of religion" (*Ummoth ha-geduroth be-darkey ha-dathoth*). By this innovative phrase, coined by Ha-Meiri, the moral and judicial institutions of Christianity and Islam and their recognition of God should be acknowledged, and their legal consequences enacted. Halacha can raise fences and pull them down. Against the winds of convention that clung to the segregative laws of the Talmud, Ha-Meiri stated that "in our days nobody heeds these things, neither Gaon, rabbi, Disciple, Hasid nor would-be Hasid."[9]

> The unitive elements of all religions are embedded in the collective conscience of each faith. Moral conscience lies at the depth of earnest interfaith dialogue.

Ha-Meiri's arguments were legal and philosophical, but the basic motivation for his radical rulings was moral sensibility sustained by a recognition that times have changed, and with them halacha has the capacity and duty to change. In breaking down the walls that isolated Jews and non-Jews, Ha-Meiri transcended the conventional method of halachic thinking. He exemplified the moral teleology of halacha that moved closer to Kook's dream.[10]

What Can Religion Do?

Stanley Milgram's and Philip Zimbardo's scientific social experiments of obedience to authority described in the previous chapter demonstrate how ordinary good people can turn into sadistic torturers under certain circumstances. In this way, cultures of conformity can dehumanize good human beings. The "banality of evil"[11] testifies to the transformation of ordinary persons holding ordinary jobs into monstrous creatures. Can religion conversely turn ordinary people into moral, disobedient protestors against cruelty and defenders of the innocent? Goodness is as banal as evil. Can ordinary people learn to do extraordinary good? Can religion counter repressive culture with a nurturing conscience? What role can moral dissent and disobedience rightly play in the religious culture of obedience?

The Pedagogy of Conscience

Conscience is developed in our formative years. Children ask questions about fairness, and questions of fairness are the birth pangs of conscience. Whether children continue to ask questions depends on whether and how they are answered.

Children's questions typically ask for "because" answers: "Why can't I stay up late?" "Why can't I go out with these friends?" "Why must I go to religious services?" "Why do I have to share my gifts with my sisters?" If the tone of the "because" answers is based on the force of authority alone—for example, "Because I said so," "Because the Bible said so," "Because the Rabbis said so," "Because God said so"—it will discourage further questions. "Because" is not an answer. The dignity of the question deserves a dignified answer. The question can be dismissed as impudence to authority or as a tribute to moral maturity. Questions are prematurely aborted by a sharp answer or a condescending silence.

Questions are the first steps toward building freedom of conscience. A primary model of the

> Encouraging questions and treating them with respect is basic for the growth of conscience.

central role of the question is evident in the Passover celebration of freedom. In the Book of Exodus, the Bible anticipates that children will ask questions. The four questions are the ritual opening of our seder, without which the Passover narrative cannot begin. The Talmud teaches that should someone not be able to be at the family seder, the lone person is to ask questions of himself or herself. Questioning is a sign of human liberation, the spiral question mark an instrument with which the armor of human bondage may be pierced. Slaves do not ask questions, and masters do not offer answers. Underlings do not ask why an act should be done or why an order is to be carried out. Slaves bite their tongues, lower their eyes before their masters, and do what they are told. Subordinates know only the unquestioning duty to obey.

Encouraging questions and treating them with respect is basic for the growth of conscience. In this, the Passover Haggadah exemplifies a model pedagogy for nurturing conscience. The sages who wrote the Haggadah understood that there are different questions and different kinds of people who ask them, and that each is to be answered respectfully, according to his or her ability. By tradition, the youngest is the first to ask the question, because it is the youngest who is the most muted in the hierarchy of the family.

Questions that cultivate conscience must not be answered with anger. The wicked son, the disobedient *rasha* who dares to ask, "What does this service mean to you?" is told that since he has excluded himself from the community (by saying "you" instead of "us"), he has thus denied the foundation of his faith. The Haggadah regrettably adds that such an arrogant questioner is to have his teeth blunted. Blunting the teeth may well shut up the dissenter, but it more likely will stunt his questioning conscience, solidifying his separation from the community. The child's teeth ought not to be blunted, nor should he be threatened with exclusion from the community. The question must be patiently answered, over and again, with words, songs, symbols, and the taste of bitter herbs of slavery and the saltwater tears of the oppressed linking the disobedient with his ancestral conscience.

> The cultivation and evolution of moral conscience are transmitted by the habits of hand and heart.

The Habit of Conscience

The ritual of asking questions at the Passover seder is a habit, and habit is one of the strongest ways through which moral conscience is trained and transmitted. The Greek term *ethike* is formed by a slight variation from the word *ethos,* which means "habit." The philosopher Aristotle took note of the habit of goodness.

Aristotle maintained that none of the moral virtues arise in us by nature. We gain virtues by exercising them, much as we gain skills by doing them—for example, men become builders of buildings by building them. "So we become just by doing just acts, temperate by doing temperate acts, brave by doing brave acts." Toward other people we become just or unjust by "doing the acts that we do in the presence of danger, and being habituated to feel confident we become brave or cowardly."[12] How early or how late are the virtues of habit formed? Aristotle answers, "It makes no small difference then whether we form habits of one kind or another from our very youth; it makes very great difference, or rather all the difference."[13]

A gradual and continually evolving pedagogy nurtures human moral sensibility. Ordinary acts, such as giving up a seat in a crowded subway to an older or disabled person, helping an impaired person across the street, holding open an elevator door to allow an individual to enter, and contributing food with kindness to a beggar, are acts of habit that inform the character of Jewish sensibility.

Conscience has its sacred rituals. In the daily morning services, the prayer book includes a section from the Talmud (Sabbath 127a) that enumerates the habits of personal acts of kindness called *gmilut hasadim*. Among these are deeds of lovingkindness that include attending the house of study morning and evening; providing hospitality; visiting the sick; helping the needy bride; attending the dead; and making peace between one person and another and between husband and wife. The habituation of ethics is reinforced by a people's rituals that designate the times and ways of sanctifying our lives. The cultivation and evolution of moral conscience are transmitted by the habits of hand and heart.

Heroes of Conscience

There is a rude question to be answered. Why should our children, or we ourselves, care about the submerged community, those singled out in the Bible: the poor, the orphaned, the stranger in our midst? Intellectual and pragmatic arguments (e.g., ignoring the plight of the poor is a threat to our people and our prosperity) do not touch the heart, hand, or spine.

Conscience, empathy, feeling the plight of the fragile, and defending the cause of the wronged are the root rationales for caring for the dispossessed. Conscience is developed through habits and through tales of our ancestry and the heroes

> Ethical character develops gradually. It begins early in our life with minor actions.

of conscience they choose to acclaim. Conscience needs heroes of flesh and blood to be emulated as witnesses to our faith.

The heroes of conscience do not wish to be idealized, nor should they be. To idealize the rescuers of the Holocaust, for example, sets them beyond the reach of ordinary men and women. To idealize them as superhuman agents places them beyond the reach of emulation. When altruists are lionized, ordinary people see themselves as hapless sheep. The perfect becomes the enemy of the good. Altruistic behavior of conscience is incremental, built step by step, precept by precept, line by line, act by act.

Conscience does not descend upon us as a lightning epiphany. Ethical character develops gradually. It begins early in our life with minor actions. The sages counsel, "Be as attentive to a minor *mitzvah* as a major one, for you do not know the reward for each of the *mitzvoth*" (*Ethics of the Fathers* 2:1).

There are degrees of acts of kindness that prepare the heart for greater deeds of goodness. Giving a piece of bread to the hungry is not the same as hiding a person hunted by the Nazis during the Holocaust. And yet the gift of a piece of bread can sustain more than the body. Primo Levi, in his book *Survival in Auschwitz*, speaks of Lorenzo, a non-Jewish Italian worker who brought Primo a piece of bread and the remainder of his rations every day in Auschwitz. That piece of bread revived Levi's faith. As he wrote later:

I believe it was really due to Lorenzo that I am alive today. It is not so much because of his material aid as for his constantly reminding by his presence, by his nature and plain manner, that there still exists a just world outside our own, something and someone still pure and whole, not corrupt and savage. Thanks to Lorenzo, I managed not to forget that I myself was a man.[14]

All this from a simple piece of bread.

Transmitting Conscience

Conscience does not appear out of the clouds as a spontaneous, celestial eruption. It begins at home, in the playpen, around family table-talk. It may be enhanced from the pulpit, from behind the pulpit, and the school desk. Conscience is the interaction in the moral dialogue between God and the children of God.

Every time hateful speech is heard against members of any race, ethnicity, or religion that goes unanswered deforms the integrity of conscience.

Every time the *shibboleth* "sticks and stones will break my bones but names will never harm me" is challenged by the observation that slander and libel ruined the spirit, conscience is served. Let us recall our tradition, "The tongue is a sharpened arrow" (Jer. 9:7). Once the arrow is released, once the tongue is released, it cannot be called back.

Every time a Jew concludes his or her prayer with the petition, "My God, guard my tongue from evil, and my lips from speaking guild," conscience is upheld. Every time the alibi is used by adolescent or adult, "But everyone does it," and is answered that that is no reason to follow the crowd, conscience is strengthened.

Every time exorbitant spending is planned to celebrate rites of passage and someone explains that it is wrong to be so profligate when so many people are hungry and without shelter, and that our expenses must be limited so as to offer our tithes to the

poor and orphaned, conscience is reinvigorated. And when someone argues that "we can afford it," someone who argues that our
self-aggrandizement is demeaning, their conscience is bolstered.

Every time that someone joins a cause to elevate health and
life, conscience is raised up.

Every time a text is studied and its moral implications are
emphasized with compassion, Torah is properly taught, and conscience informed.

Conscience calls for the preparation of the heart and the
mind and the tongue. The transmission of conscience from generation to generation rests in the hands of parents and teachers.
Conscience has many sources, but its major wellspring comes
from the home. A passage in the Talmud states it clearly:
"Whoever can stop his household from doing something bad
and does nothing is seized for his silence. If one can prevent his
fellow men from doing bad and does nothing, diminishes the
world" (Sabbath 54b). Conscience begins at home, but it
extends to the entirety of civilization.

The Many Faces of Conscience

No faith holds a monopoly on conscience. The varieties of conscience derive from many sources—secular and religious—and are
personified by heroic models from different backgrounds:
Mahatma Gandhi and Martin Buber, Martin Luther King Jr.
and Leo Baeck, Henry David Thoreau and Abraham Joshua
Heschel, Mother Teresa and Mordecai Kaplan. However varied the
origins of their conscience, they exhibit a transcendent inner character beyond denominations, dogmas, doctrines, and catechisms.

Participants in the community of conscience reveal a family resemblance: an intuitive conviction as to what is good and
what is evil; a compassion for the exploited; a courage to protect
the innocent and oppose the callous and the cruel. Each story
of conscience has its own history of trial, derision, and irrepressible determination.

One compelling story of determinative conscience is told of Henry David Thoreau, the lifelong abolitionist who lectured openly against the government's Fugitive Slave Law, defended the abolitionist John Brown, and opposed the Mexican-American War. On July 25, 1846, Thoreau ran into his old friend Sam Staples, the town's local tax collector. Staples asked Thoreau to pay for his six years of delinquent poll taxes. Thoreau refused to pay because, as he explained, he would not support a war that spread slavery's territory into Mexico. Staples pleaded with him:

> I understand your opposition. If you cannot find the money, I would be happy to lend it to you. But the law is the law, and if you refuse, I must arrest you and put you in prison. Henry, understand that I have no alternative.

Thoreau answered forthrightly: "Yes you have, Sam. You can resign your job." When Ralph Waldo Emerson, a close friend of Thoreau, visited him in jail, he asked Thoreau, "What in the world, Henry, are you doing in here?" Thoreau answered, "And what in the world, Ralph, are you doing out there?"[15]

Conscience demands courage. There is always an alternative to complicity with tyranny. In whatever language, the voice of conscience cries out loud against the threats and allurements of submissive obedience. The prophet Jeremiah confessed the bittersweet contest within conscience:

> You enticed me, O Lord, and I was enticed; You overpowered me and You prevailed. I have become a constant laughing stock. Everyone jeers at me. Every time I speak, I must cry out, must shout, "Lawlessness and rapine," for the word of the Lord causes me constant disgrace and contempt. I thought I will not mention Him, nor will I speak in His name, but His word was like a raging fire in my heart, shut up in my bones. I cannot hold it in. I was helpless. (Jer. 20:27)

Civilization cannot endure without conscience. With the death of conscience, civilization is imperiled. Conscience has many foes and many obstacles. But as the prophets of all ages testify, conscience is irrepressible. That blessed obduracy is the hope of our moral sanity and survival.

The Pendulum of Duty

I view the Jewish tradition as a pendulum swinging from the duty to obey to the duty to disobey and back. Ideally, the pendulum moves freely between the two polarities. Should the swing of the pendulum be arrested at one place, it would disrupt the flow of its arc. To release the pendulum from its stationary position calls for a sense of balance. Not to free the pendulum from its immobility is to lose the vitality and richness of the tradition. The arrested pendulum is stuck either on the right of authoritarianism or on the left of anarchy.

In our time, the pendulum is frozen on the right side. An overall view of religion, politics, and ethics suggests the overwhelming bias toward the duty to obey. It disproportionately favors authoritative religion and authoritative polices of the state.

From the time of the Nazi Holocaust until this day, more than fifty genocides and politicides have taken place, at a cost of at least 12 million soldiers and as many as 26 million civilian lives. The international community has become habituated to Holocaust complacency.[16] A contagious complicity and conformity have paralyzed the moral will of civilized countries. The conscience of civilization wanes. Conformity, whether religious or secular, has become the badge of piety and patriotism. The pendulum of duty has been arrested. It requires wisdom, mutual respect, and largeness of spirit to embrace both duties: both the law and conscience, both the external commands and the internal moral imperatives.

NOTES

Introduction

1. Baruch Spinoza, *Tractatus Theologico-Politicus* (1670), cited in Abraham Joshua Heschel, *God in Search of Man: A Philosophy of Judaism* (Philadelphia: Jewish Publication Society, 1964), p. xiii.
2. T. S. Eliot, *The Rock*, in the opening stanza of "Choruses from the Rock."

Chapter 1

1. *Oroth Ha Kodesh*, "The Lights of Holiness," 3 vols. (Jerusalem: Agudah Le Hotzaot Sifre Ha Rav Kook, 1950).
2. Abraham J. Heschel, *God in Search of Man: A Philosophy of Judaism* (New York: Farrar, Straus and Giroux, 1955), p. 158.

Chapter 2

1. Rabbi Arthur A. Cohen, ed., "Can Religious Law Be Immoral?" in *A Perspective on Jews and Judaism* (New York: The Rabbinical Assembly, 1978), p. 165
2. Rabbi Arthur A. Cohen and Paul Mendes-Flohr, eds., *Commandment and Contemporary Jewish Religious Thought* (New York: Scribners, 1987), p. 72.
3. Michael Wyschograd, *Standing before God* (Jersey City, NJ: KTAV, 1986).
4. Moses Maimonides, *Mishnah Torah Sanhedrin* (XII, 2), Yale Judaica Series (New Haven, CT: Yale University Press, 1951).
5. ———, The Book of Acquisitions 9:81.
6. ———, The Book of Seasons: Sabbath 2:3.

7. "God, Torah and Israel," in Abraham Joshua Heschel, *Moral Grandeur and Spiritual Audacity* (New York: Farrar, Straus and Giroux, 1996), p. 196; and his Yiddish work on his Hassidic work, *Kotz: The Struggle for Integrity* (Tel Aviv: Hamenorah Publishing House, 1973).

8. Nechama Leibowitz, *Studies in Vayikra (Leviticus)* (New York: World Zionist Organization, 1980), p. 173–174.

9. Talmud, Pesachim 22b, and Maimonides's *Homicide and the Preservation of Life*, 12:14.

10. Morris Raphael Cohen, *A Dreamer's Journey* (Boston: Beacon Press, 1949).

Chapter 3

1. Aristotle, *Nicomachean Ethics*, Chapter 10, pp. 11–73.

2. A philosophical novel based on the story of the king of Khazaria, a kingdom located between the Black Sea and Caspian Sea. In the eighth century the king of Khazaria, undecided whether he should affiliate with the Christians or Muslims, had great scholars argue before him the merits of the world's religions, and as a result of this debate converted to Judaism as did a portion of his country. The *Kuzari* recreates the debate before the king.

3. Hyman Goldin, ed., *Hamdrich* (Chatham, NY: Hebrew Publishing Company, 1956), pp. 126–127.

4. Rabbi Joseph B. Soloveitchik, *The Lonely Man of Faith* (Chatham, NY: Hebrew Publishing Company, 1956), pp. 60–61.

5. T. S. Eliot, *The Cocktail Party* (Hollywood, CA: Samuel French, Inc., 1950), p. 88.

6. Maurice Friedman and Paul Arthur Schilpp, "Samuel and Agag," in *The Philosophy of Martin Buber* (La Salle: Open Court Publishing, 1967), p. 31.

7. Paul Mendes-Flohr, *Divided Passions: Jewish Intellectuals and the Experience of Modernity* (Detroit: Wayne State University Press, 1991), pp. 345–346.

8. Martin Buber, *Eclipse of God: Studies in the Relation between Religion and Philosophy* (New York: Harper, 1952), p. 86.

Chapter 4

1. Fyodor Dostoevsky, *The Brothers Karamozov*, cited in *The Existential Imagination*, edited by Frederick Karl and Leo Hamilton (Robbinsdale, MN: Fawcet Publications, 1963), p. 66.

2. Michael T. Ghiselin, *The Economy of Nature and the Evolution of Sex* (Berkeley, CA: University of California Press, 1974).

3. Sigmund Freud, *Civilization and Its Discontents*, translated and edited by James Strachey (New York: W.W. Norton, 1961), p. 58.

4. Quoted in Robert E. Fitch, "Secular Images of Man in Contemporary Literature," in *Religious Education* (LIII), 1958, p. 87.

5. George Santayana, *Dominations and Power: Reflections on Liberty, Society, and Government* (New York: Scribners, 1951).

6. Friedrich Nietzsche, *On the Genealogy of Morals*, cited in *The Philosophy of Nietzsche* (New York: The Modern Library, 1937).

7. Ibid., p. 643.

8. Thomas Robert Malthus, *An Essay on the Principle of Population as it Affects the Future Improvement of Society* (1798).

9. Herbert Spencer, "The Sins of Legislators," in *The Man Versus the State.*

10. *The Descent of Man*, cited by Frans de Wahl in *Primates and Philosophers* (Princeton, NJ: Princeton University Press, 2006).

11. Karl Barth, *Church Dogmatics*, Vol. 2.

12. Abraham Joshua Heschel, *God in Search of Man: A Philosophy of Judaism* (New York: Farrar, Straus and Giroux, 1955), p. 298.

13. Martin Buber, *Eclipse of God* (New York: Harper, 1952), pp. 117–120.

Chapter 5

1. Heschel's conviction is articulated in two of his addresses: "Children and Youth" and "Jewish Education" in his *The Insecurity of Freedom* (New York: Schocken Books, 1960), pp. 39, 223.

2. Philip Zimbardo, *The Lucifer Effect* (New York: Random House, 2007), p. 12; Jonathan Sacks, *The Dignity of Difference* (London: Continuum International Publishing, 2003), p. 4.

3. Martin Gilbert, "The Righteous," in *Perspectives: Autumn 2004*, p. 6.

4. I am especially indebted to the scholarly works of Nechama Tec, *When Light Pierced the Darkness* (New York: Oxford University Press, 1986); Mordechai Paldiel, *Diplomat Heroes of the Holocaust* (Jersey City, NJ: KTAV, 2007); and Philip Friedman, *Their Brothers' Keepers* (New York: Crown, 1952).

5. Tec, *When Light Pierced the Darkness*, p. 76.

6. Philip Friedman, *Their Brothers' Keepers* (New York: Crown, 1957), p. 26.

7. Kovner was a member of *Hashomer Hatzair,* a socialist Zionist youth movement.
8. Friedman, *Their Brothers' Keepers,* p. 27
9. Paldiel, *Diplomat Heroes of the Holocaust.*
10. Ibid., p 74.
11. Ibid., p. 76.
12. Ibid., p. 77.
13. Ibid., p. 82–83.
14. Ibid., p. 83.
15. Ibid., p. 56.
16. Ibid., p. 59–60.

Chapter 6

1. Tec, *When Light Pierced the Darkness,* p. 110–112
2. Zofia Kossak-Szczucka, "The Protest," cited in Tec, *When Light Pierced the Darkness* (New York: Oxford University Press, 1986), p. 110–12.
3. Ibid., p. 111–112.
4. Ibid.
5. Gilbert, "The Righteous," in *Perspectives: Autumn 2004,* pp. 6–11.

Chapter 7

1. Rudolf Hess, *Fuehrer: You Order, We Obey.*
2. Ibid.
3. Martin Gilbert, *Nuremberg Diary* (New York: Farrar, Straus, 1947).
4. Zimbardo, *The Lucifer Effect,* p. 30–33.
5. Stanley Milgram, *Obedience to Authority: An Experimental View* (New York: Harper Perennial), 1983, p. xii.
6. Ibid.
7. Ibid., p. 6.

Chapter 8

1. Robert Bretall, ed., *"Either/Or," A Kierkegaard Anthology* (Princeton, NJ: Princeton University Press, 1946), p. 19.
2. Rashi on Ketuboth 57a.
3. The essence and purpose of halachic law is masterfully discussed by Eliezer Berkovits in *Not in Heaven: The Nature and Function of Halakha* (Jersey City, NJ: KTAV, 1983).
4. *The Pangs of Cleansing,* in Ben Zion Bokser's translation of Kook's *The Rights of Penitence* (Mahwah, NJ: Paulist Press, 1978), p. 9.

5. Abraham Isaac Kook, *Oroth Ha Kodesh*, "The Lights of Holiness," 3 vols. (Jerusalem: Agudah Le Hotzaot Sifre Ha Rav Kook, 1950), p. 264.

6. Ibid., p. 265.

7. Abraham Isaac Kook, *The Lights of Penitence, The Moral Principles, Lights of Holiness, Essays, Letters and Poems*, translated by Ben Zion Bokser (New York: Paulist Press, 1978), p. 12.

8. Abraham Isaac Kook, *Igrot Rayanah*, Vol. 1, letter 194, Jerusalem, 1943.

9. Jacob Katz, *Exclusiveness and Tolerance: Studies in Jewish-Gentile Relations in Medieval and Modern Times* (New York: Schocken Books, 1962), pp. 114–120.

10. Ha-Meiri's *Beth Ha-Behirah* on Avodah Zara, as cited in Jacob Katz's *Exclusiveness and Tolerance* (New York: Schocken Books, 1961), p. 116

11. Hannah Arendt, *Eichmann in Jerusalem: A Report on the Banality of Evil* (New York: Viking, 1963).

12. Aristotle, *Nicomachean Ethics*, Book 2, 1103.

13. Ibid.

14. Primo Levi, *If This Is a Man* (New York: Random House/Everyman's Library, 2000).

15. *Civil Disobedience: Theory and Practice*, Hugo A. Bedau, ed., (New York: Macmillan, 1969), p. 7–8.

16. Barbara Harff, "No Lessons Learned from the Holocaust?" in *American Political Science Review* 97:1 (February 2003), p. 57.

Bar/Bat Mitzvah

The JGirl's Guide: The Young Jewish Woman's Handbook for Coming of Age
By Penina Adelman, Ali Feldman, and Shulamit Reinharz
This inspirational, interactive guidebook helps pre-teen Jewish girls address the many issues surrounding coming of age.   6 x 9, 240 pp, Quality PB, 978-1-58023-215-9 **$14.99**
  Also Available: **The JGirl's Teacher's and Parent's Guide**
  8½ x 11, 56 pp, PB, 978-1-58023-225-8 **$8.99**

Bar/Bat Mitzvah Basics: A Practical Family Guide to Coming of Age Together
Edited by Cantor Helen Leneman   6 x 9, 240 pp, Quality PB, 978-1-58023-151-0 **$18.95**

The Bar/Bat Mitzvah Memory Book, 2nd Edition: An Album for Treasuring the Spiritual Celebration *By Rabbi Jeffrey K. Salkin and Nina Salkin*
8 x 10, 48 pp, Deluxe HC, 2-color text, ribbon marker, 978-1-58023-263-0 **$19.99**

For Kids—Putting God on Your Guest List, 2nd Edition: How to Claim the Spiritual Meaning of Your Bar or Bat Mitzvah *By Rabbi Jeffrey K. Salkin*
6 x 9, 144 pp, Quality PB, 978-1-58023-308-8 **$15.99** *For ages 11–13*

Putting God on the Guest List, 3rd Edition: How to Reclaim the Spiritual Meaning of Your Child's Bar or Bat Mitzvah *By Rabbi Jeffrey K. Salkin*
6 x 9, 224 pp, Quality PB, 978-1-58023-222-7 **$16.99**; HC, 978-1-58023-260-9 **$24.99**
  Also Available: **Putting God on the Guest List Teacher's Guide**
  8½ x 11, 48 pp, PB, 978-1-58023-226-5 **$8.99**

Tough Questions Jews Ask: A Young Adult's Guide to Building a Jewish Life
By Rabbi Edward Feinstein   6 x 9, 160 pp, Quality PB, 978-1-58023-139-8 **$14.99** *For ages 12 & up*
  Also Available: **Tough Questions Jews Ask Teacher's Guide**
  8½ x 11, 72 pp, PB, 978-1-58023-187-9 **$8.95**

Bible Study/Midrash

Abraham's Bind & Other Bible Tales of Trickery, Folly, Mercy and Love *By Michael J. Caduto*
Re-imagines many biblical characters, retelling their stories.
6 x 9, 224 pp, HC, 978-1-59473-186-0 **$19.99** *(A SkyLight Paths book)*

Ancient Secrets: Using the Stories of the Bible to Improve Our Everyday Lives
By Rabbi Levi Meier, PhD 5½ x 8½, 288 pp, Quality PB, 978-1-58023-064-3 **$16.95**

The Genesis of Leadership: What the Bible Teaches Us about Vision, Values and Leading Change *By Rabbi Nathan Laufer; Foreword by Senator Joseph I. Lieberman*
Unlike other books on leadership, this one is rooted in the stories of the Bible.
6 x 9, 288 pp, Quality PB, 978-1-58023-352-1 **$18.99**; HC, 978-1-58023-241-8 **$24.99**

Hineini in Our Lives: Learning How to Respond to Others through 14 Biblical Texts and Personal Stories *By Norman J. Cohen*   6 x 9, 240 pp, Quality PB, 978-1-58023-274-6 **$16.99**

Moses and the Journey to Leadership: Timeless Lessons of Effective Management from the Bible and Today's Leaders *By Dr. Norman J. Cohen*
6 x 9, 240 pp, Quality PB, 978-1-58023-351-4 **$18.99**; HC, 978-1-58023-227-2 **$21.99**

Self, Struggle & Change: Family Conflict Stories in Genesis and Their Healing Insights for Our Lives *By Norman J. Cohen*   6 x 9, 224 pp, Quality PB, 978-1-879045-66-8 **$18.99**

The Triumph of Eve & Other Subversive Bible Tales *By Matt Biers-Ariel*
5½ x 8½, 192 pp, Quality PB, 978-1-59473-176-1 **$14.99**; HC, 978-1-59473-040-5 **$19.99**
(A SkyLight Paths book)

The Wisdom of Judaism: An Introduction to the Values of the Talmud
By Rabbi Dov Peretz Elkins
Explores the essence of Judaism.   6 x 9, 192 pp, Quality PB, 978-1-58023-327-9 **$16.99**
  Also Available: **The Wisdom of Judaism Teacher's Guide**
  8½ x 11, 18 pp, PB, 978-1-58023-350-7 **$8.99**

Or phone, fax, mail or e-mail to: **JEWISH LIGHTS Publishing**
Sunset Farm Offices, Route 4 • P.O. Box 237 • Woodstock, Vermont 05091
Tel: (802) 457-4000 • Fax: (802) 457-4004 • www.jewishlights.com
Credit card orders: (800) 962-4544 (8:30AM–5:30PM ET Monday–Friday)
Generous discounts on quantity orders. SATISFACTION GUARANTEED. Prices subject to change.

Congregation Resources

The Art of Public Prayer, 2nd Edition: Not for Clergy Only *By Lawrence A. Hoffman*
6 x 9, 272 pp, Quality PB, 978-1-893361-06-5 **$19.99** *(A SkyLight Paths book)*

Becoming a Congregation of Learners: Learning as a Key to Revitalizing
Congregational Life *By Isa Aron, PhD; Foreword by Rabbi Lawrence A. Hoffman*
6 x 9, 304 pp, Quality PB, 978-1-58023-089-6 **$19.95**

Finding a Spiritual Home: How a New Generation of Jews Can Transform the
American Synagogue *By Rabbi Sidney Schwarz*
6 x 9, 352 pp, Quality PB, 978-1-58023-185-5 **$19.95**

Jewish Pastoral Care, 2nd Edition: A Practical Handbook from Traditional &
Contemporary Sources *Edited by Rabbi Dayle A. Friedman*
6 x 9, 528 pp, HC, 978-1-58023-221-0 **$40.00**

Jewish Spiritual Direction: An Innovative Guide from Traditional and Contemporary
Sources *Edited by Rabbi Howard A. Addison and Barbara Eve Breitman*
6 x 9, 368 pp, HC, 978-1-58023-230-2 **$30.00**

The Self-Renewing Congregation: Organizational Strategies for Revitalizing
Congregational Life *By Isa Aron, PhD; Foreword by Dr. Ron Wolfson*
6 x 9, 304 pp, Quality PB, 978-1-58023-166-4 **$19.95**

Spiritual Community: The Power to Restore Hope, Commitment and Joy
By Rabbi David A. Teutsch, PhD 5½ x 8½, 144 pp, HC, 978-1-58023-270-8 **$19.99**

The Spirituality of Welcoming: How to Transform Your Congregation into a
Sacred Community *By Dr. Ron Wolfson* 6 x 9, 224 pp, Quality PB, 978-1-58023-244-9 **$19.99**

Rethinking Synagogues: A New Vocabulary for Congregational Life
By Rabbi Lawrence A. Hoffman 6 x 9, 240 pp, Quality PB, 978-1-58023-248-7 **$19.99**

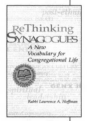

Children's Books

What You Will See Inside a Synagogue

By Rabbi Lawrence A. Hoffman and Dr. Ron Wolfson; Full-color photos by Bill Aron
A colorful, fun-to-read introduction that explains the ways and whys of Jewish
worship and religious life. 8½ x 10½, 32 pp, Full-color photos, Quality PB, 978-1-59473-256-0 **$8.99**
For ages 6 & up (A SkyLight Paths book)

The Kids' Fun Book of Jewish Time

By Emily Sper 9 x 7½, 24 pp, Full-color illus., HC, 978-1-58023-311-8 **$16.99**

In God's Hands

By Lawrence Kushner and Gary Schmidt 9 x 12, 32 pp, HC, 978-1-58023-224-1 **$16.99**

Because Nothing Looks Like God

By Lawrence and Karen Kushner
Introduces children to the possibilities of spiritual life.
11 x 8½, 32 pp, Full-color illus., HC, 978-1-58023-092-6 **$17.99** *For ages 4 & up*

Also Available: **Because Nothing Looks Like God Teacher's Guide**
8½ x 11, 22 pp, PB, 978-1-58023-140-4 **$6.95** *For ages 5–8*

Board Book Companions to *Because Nothing Looks Like God*
5 x 5, 24 pp, Full-color illus., SkyLight Paths Board Books *For ages 0–4*

What Does God Look Like? 978-1-893361-23-2 **$7.99**

How Does God Make Things Happen? 978-1-893361-24-9 **$7.95**

Where Is God? 978-1-893361-17-1 **$7.99**

The Book of Miracles: A Young Person's Guide to Jewish Spiritual Awareness
By Lawrence Kushner. All-new illustrations by the author
6 x 9, 96 pp, 2-color illus., HC, 978-1-879045-78-1 **$16.95** *For ages 9 and up*

In Our Image: God's First Creatures

By Nancy Sohn Swartz 9 x 12, 32 pp, Full-color illus., HC, 978-1-879045-99-6 **$16.95** *For ages 4 & up*

Also Available as a Board Book: **How Did the Animals Help God?**
5 x 5, 24 pp, Board, Full-color illus., 978-1-59473-044-3 **$7.99** *For ages 0–4 (A SkyLight Paths book)*

What Makes Someone a Jew?

By Lauren Seidman
Reflects the changing face of American Judaism.
10 x 8½, 32 pp, Full-color photos, Quality PB Original, 978-1-58023-321-7 **$8.99** *For ages 3–6*

Children's Books
by Sandy Eisenberg Sasso

Adam & Eve's First Sunset: God's New Day
Engaging new story explores fear and hope, faith and gratitude in ways that will delight kids and adults—inspiring us to bless each of God's days and nights.
9 x 12, 32 pp, Full-color illus., HC, 978-1-58023-177-0 **$17.95** *For ages 4 & up*

Also Available as a Board Book: **Adam and Eve's New Day**
5 x 5, 24 pp, Full-color illus., Board, 978-1-59473-205-8 **$7.99** *For ages 0–4 (A SkyLight Paths book)*

But God Remembered
Stories of Women from Creation to the Promised Land
Four different stories of women—Lillith, Serach, Bityah, and the Daughters of Z—teach us important values through their faith and actions.
9 x 12, 32 pp, Full-color illus., Quality PB, 978-1-58023-372-9 **$8.99**; HC, 978-1-879045-43-9 **$16.95** *For ages 8 & up*

Cain & Abel: Finding the Fruits of Peace
Shows children that we have the power to deal with anger in positive ways. Provides questions for kids and adults to explore together.
9 x 12, 32 pp, Full-color illus., HC, 978-1-58023-123-7 **$16.95** *For ages 5 & up*

God in Between
If you wanted to find God, where would you look? This magical, mythical tale teaches that God can be found where we are: within all of us and the relationships between us.
9 x 12, 32 pp, Full-color illus., HC, 978-1-879045-86-6 **$16.95** *For ages 4 & up*

God's Paintbrush: Special 10th Anniversary Edition
Wonderfully interactive, invites children of all faiths and backgrounds to encounter God through moments in their own lives. Provides questions adult and child can explore together.
11 x 8½, 32 pp, Full-color illus., HC, 978-1-58023-195-4 **$17.95** *For ages 4 & up*

Also Available: **God's Paintbrush Teacher's Guide**
8½ x 11, 32 pp, PB, 978-1-879045-57-6 **$8.95**

God's Paintbrush Celebration Kit
A Spiritual Activity Kit for Teachers and Students of All Faiths, All Backgrounds
Additional activity sheets available:
8-Student Activity Sheet Pack (40 sheets/5 sessions), 978-1-58023-058-2 **$19.95**
Single-Student Activity Sheet Pack (5 sessions), 978-1-58023-059-9 **$3.95**

In God's Name
Like an ancient myth in its poetic text and vibrant illustrations, this award-winning modern fable about the search for God's name celebrates the diversity and, at the same time, the unity of all people.
9 x 12, 32 pp, Full-color illus., HC, 978-1-879045-26-2 **$16.99** *For ages 4 & up*

Also Available as a Board Book: **What Is God's Name?**
5 x 5, 24 pp, Board, Full-color illus., 978-1-893361-10-2 **$7.99** *For ages 0–4 (A SkyLight Paths book)*

Also Available: **In God's Name video and study guide**
Computer animation, original music, and children's voices. 18 min. **$29.99**

Also Available in Spanish: **El nombre de Dios**
9 x 12, 32 pp, Full-color illus., HC, 978-1-893361-63-8 **$16.95** *(A SkyLight Paths book)*

Noah's Wife: The Story of Naamah
When God tells Noah to bring the animals of the world onto the ark, God also calls on Naamah, Noah's wife, to save each plant on Earth. Based on an ancient text.
9 x 12, 32 pp, Full-color illus., HC, 978-1-58023-134-3 **$16.95** *For ages 4 & up*

Also Available as a Board Book: **Naamah, Noah's Wife**
5 x 5, 24 pp, Full-color illus., Board, 978-1-893361-56-0 **$7.95** *For ages 0–4 (A SkyLight Paths book)*

For Heaven's Sake: Finding God in Unexpected Places
9 x 12, 32 pp, Full-color illus., HC, 978-1-58023-054-4 **$16.95** *For ages 4 & up*

God Said Amen: Finding the Answers to Our Prayers
9 x 12, 32 pp, Full-color illus., HC, 978-1-58023-080-3 **$16.95** *For ages 4 & up*

Meditation

The Handbook of Jewish Meditation Practices
A Guide for Enriching the Sabbath and Other Days of Your Life
By Rabbi David A. Cooper Easy-to-learn meditation techniques.
6 x 9, 208 pp, Quality PB, 978-1-58023-102-2 **$16.95**

Discovering Jewish Meditation: Instruction & Guidance for Learning an Ancient
Spiritual Practice *By Nan Fink Gefen*
6 x 9, 208 pp, Quality PB, 978-1-58023-067-4 **$16.95**

A Heart of Stillness: A Complete Guide to Learning the Art of Meditation
By David A. Cooper 5½ x 8½, 272 pp, Quality PB, 978-1-893361-03-4 **$16.95** *(A SkyLight Paths book)*

Meditation from the Heart of Judaism: Today's Teachers Share Their Practices,
Techniques, and Faith *Edited by Avram Davis*
6 x 9, 256 pp, Quality PB, 978-1-58023-049-0 **$16.95**

Silence, Simplicity & Solitude: A Complete Guide to Spiritual Retreat at Home
By David A. Cooper 5½ x 8½, 336 pp, Quality PB, 978-1-893361-04-1 **$16.95**
(A SkyLight Paths book)

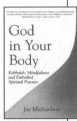

Ritual/Sacred Practice

The Jewish Dream Book: The Key to Opening the Inner Meaning of
Your Dreams *By Vanessa L. Ochs with Elizabeth Ochs; Full-color illus. by Kristina Swarner*
Instructions for how modern people can perform ancient Jewish dream practices
and dream interpretations drawn from the Jewish wisdom tradition.
8 x 8, 128 pp, Full-color illus., Deluxe PB w/flaps, 978-1-58023-132-9 **$16.95**

God in Your Body: Kabbalah, Mindfulness and Embodied Spiritual Practice
By Jay Michaelson
The first comprehensive treatment of the body in Jewish spiritual practice and an
essential guide to the sacred.
6 x 9, 288 pp, Quality PB, 978-1-58023-304-0 **$18.99**

The Book of Jewish Sacred Practices: CLAL's Guide to Everyday & Holiday
Rituals & Blessings *Edited by Rabbi Irwin Kula and Vanessa L. Ochs, PhD*
6 x 9, 368 pp, Quality PB, 978-1-58023-152-7 **$18.95**

Jewish Ritual: A Brief Introduction for Christians
By Rabbi Kerry M. Olitzky and Rabbi Daniel Judson
5½ x 8½, 144 pp, Quality PB, 978-1-58023-210-4 **$14.99**

The Rituals & Practices of a Jewish Life: A Handbook for Personal Spiritual
Renewal *Edited by Rabbi Kerry M. Olitzky and Rabbi Daniel Judson*
6 x 9, 272 pp, illus., Quality PB, 978-1-58023-169-5 **$18.95**

The Sacred Art of Lovingkindness: Preparing to Practice
By Rabbi Rami Shapiro 5½ x 8½, 176 pp, Quality PB, 978-1-59473-151-8 **$16.99**
(A SkyLight Paths book)

Science Fiction/Mystery & Detective Fiction

Mystery Midrash: An Anthology of Jewish Mystery & Detective Fiction
Edited by Lawrence W. Raphael; Preface by Joel Siegel
6 x 9, 304 pp, Quality PB, 978-1-58023-055-1 **$16.95**

Criminal Kabbalah: An Intriguing Anthology of Jewish Mystery & Detective Fiction
Edited by Lawrence W. Raphael; Foreword by Laurie R. King
6 x 9, 256 pp, Quality PB, 978-1-58023-109-1 **$16.95**

Wandering Stars: An Anthology of Jewish Fantasy & Science Fiction
Edited by Jack Dann; Introduction by Isaac Asimov
6 x 9, 272 pp, Quality PB, 978-1-58023-005-6 **$18.99**

More Wandering Stars: An Anthology of Outstanding Stories of Jewish Fantasy and
Science Fiction *Edited by Jack Dann; Introduction by Isaac Asimov*
6 x 9, 192 pp, Quality PB, 978-1-58023-063-6 **$16.95**

Inspiration

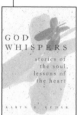

Happiness and the Human Spirit: The Spirituality of Becoming the Best You Can Be *By Abraham J. Twerski, MD*
Shows you that true happiness is attainable once you stop looking outside yourself for the source.   6 x 9, 176 pp, HC, 978-1-58023-343-9 **$19.99**

The Bridge to Forgiveness: Stories and Prayers for Finding God and Restoring Wholeness *By Rabbi Karyn D. Kedar*
Examines how forgiveness can be the bridge that connects us to wholeness and peace.
6 x 9, 176 pp, HC, 978-1-58023-324-8 **$19.99**

God's To-Do List: 103 Ways to Be an Angel and Do God's Work on Earth
By Dr. Ron Wolfson 6 x 9, 150 pp, Quality PB, 978-1-58023-301-9 **$16.99**

God in All Moments: Mystical & Practical Spiritual Wisdom from Hasidic Masters
Edited and translated by Or N. Rose with Ebn D. Leader
5½ x 8½, 192 pp, Quality PB, 978-1-58023-186-2 **$16.95**

Our Dance with God: Finding Prayer, Perspective and Meaning in the Stories of Our Lives *By Karyn D. Kedar* 6 x 9, 176 pp, Quality PB, 978-1-58023-202-9 **$16.99**
Also Available: **The Dance of the Dolphin** (HC edition of *Our Dance with God*)
6 x 9, 176 pp, HC, 978-1-58023-154-1 **$19.95**

The Empty Chair: Finding Hope and Joy—Timeless Wisdom from a Hasidic Master, Rebbe Nachman of Breslov *Adapted by Moshe Mykoff and the Breslov Research Institute*
4 x 6, 128 pp, 2-color text, Deluxe PB w/flaps, 978-1-879045-67-5 **$9.99**

The Gentle Weapon: Prayers for Everyday and Not-So-Everyday Moments—Timeless Wisdom from the Teachings of the Hasidic Master, Rebbe Nachman of Breslov
Adapted by Moshe Mykoff and S. C. Mizrahi, together with the Breslov Research Institute
4 x 6, 144 pp, 2-color text, Deluxe PB w/flaps, 978-1-58023-022-3 **$9.99**

God Whispers: Stories of the Soul, Lessons of the Heart *By Karyn D. Kedar*
6 x 9, 176 pp, Quality PB, 978-1-58023-088-9 **$15.95**

Restful Reflections: Nighttime Inspiration to Calm the Soul, Based on Jewish Wisdom
By Rabbi Kerry M. Olitzky & Rabbi Lori Forman 4½ x 6½, 448 pp, Quality PB, 978-1-58023-091-9 **$15.95**

Sacred Intentions: Daily Inspiration to Strengthen the Spirit, Based on Jewish Wisdom
By Rabbi Kerry M. Olitzky and Rabbi Lori Forman 4½ x 6½, 448 pp, Quality PB, 978-1-58023-061-2 **$15.95**

Kabbalah/Mysticism/Enneagram

Awakening to Kabbalah: The Guiding Light of Spiritual Fulfillment
By Rav Michael Laitman, PhD 6 x 9, 192 pp, HC, 978-1-58023-264-7 **$21.99**

Seek My Face: A Jewish Mystical Theology *By Arthur Green*
6 x 9, 304 pp, Quality PB, 978-1-58023-130-5 **$19.95**

Zohar: Annotated & Explained
Translation and annotation by Daniel C. Matt; Foreword by Andrew Harvey
5½ x 8½, 176 pp, Quality PB, 978-1-893361-51-5 **$15.99**   *(A SkyLight Paths book)*

Ehyeh: A Kabbalah for Tomorrow
By Arthur Green 6 x 9, 224 pp, Quality PB, 978-1-58023-213-5 **$16.99**

The Flame of the Heart: Prayers of a Chasidic Mystic *By Reb Noson of Breslov. Translated by David Sears with the Breslov Research Institute* 5 x 7¼, 160 pp, Quality PB, 978-1-58023-246-3 **$15.99**

The Gift of Kabbalah: Discovering the Secrets of Heaven, Renewing Your Life on Earth
By Tamar Frankiel, PhD 6 x 9, 256 pp, Quality PB, 978-1-58023-141-1 **$16.95;**
HC, 978-1-58023-108-4 **$21.95**

Kabbalah: A Brief Introduction for Christians
By Tamar Frankiel, PhD 5½ x 8½, 208 pp, Quality PB, 978-1-58023-303-3 **$16.99**

The Lost Princess and Other Kabbalistic Tales of Rebbe Nachman of Breslov
The Seven Beggars and Other Kabbalistic Tales of Rebbe Nachman of Breslov
Translated by Rabbi Aryeh Kaplan; Preface by Rabbi Chaim Kramer
Lost Princess: 6 x 9, 400 pp, Quality PB, 978-1-58023-217-3 **$18.99**
Seven Beggars: 6 x 9, 192 pp, Quality PB, 978-1-58023-250-0 **$16.99**

See also *The Way Into Jewish Mystical Tradition* in Spirituality / The Way Into... Series

Current Events/History

A Dream of Zion: American Jews Reflect on Why Israel Matters to Them
Edited by Rabbi Jeffrey K. Salkin Explores what Jewish people in America have to say about Israel. 6 x 9, 304 pp, HC, 978-1-58023-340-8 **$24.99**
Also Available: **A Dream of Zion Teacher's Guide** 8½ x 11, 18 pp, PB, 978-1-58023-356-9 **$8.99**

The Jewish Connection to Israel, the Promised Land: A Brief Introduction for Christians *By Rabbi Eugene Korn, PhD* 5½ x 8½, 192 pp, Quality PB, 978-1-58023-318-7 **$14.99**

The Story of the Jews: A 4,000-Year Adventure—A Graphic History Book
Written & illustrated by Stan Mack 6 x 9, 288 pp, illus., Quality PB, 978-1-58023-155-8 **$16.99**

Hannah Senesh: Her Life and Diary, the First Complete Edition
By Hannah Senesh; Foreword by Marge Piercy; Preface by Eitan Senesh
6 x 9, 368 pp, Quality PB, 978-1-58023-342-2 **$19.99**; 352 pp, HC, 978-1-58023-212-8 **$24.99**

The Ethiopian Jews of Israel: Personal Stories of Life in the Promised
Land *By Len Lyons, PhD; Foreword by Alan Dershowitz; Photographs by Ilan Ossendryver*
Recounts, through photographs and words, stories of Ethiopian Jews.
10½ x 10, 240 pp, 100 full-color photos, HC, 978-1-58023-323-1 **$34.99**

Foundations of Sephardic Spirituality: The Inner Life of Jews of the Ottoman Empire
By Rabbi Marc D. Angel, PhD 6 x 9, 224 pp, HC, 978-1-58023-243-2 **$24.99**

Judaism and Justice: The Jewish Passion to Repair the World
By Rabbi Sidney Schwarz 6 x 9, 352 pp, Quality PB, 978-1-58023-353-8 **$19.99**

Ecology/Environment

A Wild Faith: Jewish Ways into Wilderness, Wilderness Ways into Judaism
By Rabbi Mike Comins; Foreword by Nigel Savage
Offers ways to enliven and deepen your spiritual life through wilderness experience.
6 x 9, 240 pp, Quality PB, 978-1-58023-316-3 **$16.99**

Ecology & the Jewish Spirit: Where Nature & the Sacred Meet
Edited by Ellen Bernstein 6 x 9, 288 pp, Quality PB, 978-1-58023-082-7 **$18.99**

Torah of the Earth: Exploring 4,000 Years of Ecology in Jewish Thought
Vol. 1: Biblical Israel: One Land, One People; Rabbinic Judaism: One People, Many Lands
Vol. 2: Zionism: One Land, Two Peoples; Eco-Judaism: One Earth, Many Peoples
Edited by Arthur Waskow Vol. 1: 6 x 9, 272 pp, Quality PB, 978-1-58023-086-5 **$19.95**
Vol. 2: 6 x 9, 336 pp, Quality PB, 978-1-58023-087-2 **$19.95**

The Way Into Judaism and the Environment
By Jeremy Benstein 6 x 9, 224 pp, HC, 978-1-58023-268-5 **$24.99**

Grief/Healing

Healing and the Jewish Imagination: Spiritual and Practical
Perspectives on Judaism and Health *Edited by Rabbi William Cutter, PhD*
Explores Judaism for comfort in times of illness and perspectives on suffering.
6 x 9, 240 pp, HC, 978-1-58023-314-9 **$24.99**

Grief in Our Seasons: A Mourner's Kaddish Companion *By Rabbi Kerry M. Olitzky*
4½ x 6½, 448 pp, Quality PB, 978-1-879045-55-2 **$15.95**

Healing of Soul, Healing of Body: Spiritual Leaders Unfold the Strength & Solace
in Psalms *Edited by Rabbi Simkha Y. Weintraub, CSW*
6 x 9, 128 pp, 2-color illus. text, Quality PB, 978-1-879045-31-6 **$14.99**

Mourning & Mitzvah, 2nd Edition: A Guided Journal for Walking the Mourner's
Path through Grief to Healing *By Anne Brener, LCSW*
7½ x 9, 304 pp, Quality PB, 978-1-58023-113-8 **$19.99**

Tears of Sorrow, Seeds of Hope, 2nd Edition: A Jewish Spiritual Companion for
Infertility and Pregnancy Loss *By Rabbi Nina Beth Cardin*
6 x 9, 208 pp, Quality PB, 978-1-58023-233-3 **$18.99**

A Time to Mourn, a Time to Comfort, 2nd Edition: A Guide to Jewish
Bereavement *By Dr. Ron Wolfson*
7 x 9, 384 pp, Quality PB, 978-1-58023-253-1 **$19.99**

When a Grandparent Dies: A Kid's Own Remembering Workbook for Dealing
with Shiva and the Year Beyond *By Nechama Liss-Levinson, PhD*
8 x 10, 48 pp, 2-color text, HC, 978-1-879045-44-6 **$15.95** *For ages 7–13*

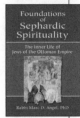

Holidays/Holy Days

Rosh Hashanah Readings: Inspiration, Information and Contemplation
Yom Kippur Readings: Inspiration, Information and Contemplation
Edited by Rabbi Dov Peretz Elkins with Section Introductions from Arthur Green's These Are the Words
An extraordinary collection of readings, prayers and insights that enable the modern worshiper to enter into the spirit of the High Holy Days in a personal and powerful way, permitting the meaning of the Jewish New Year to enter the heart.
RHR: 6 x 9, 400 pp, HC, 978-1-58023-239-5 **$24.99**
YKR: 6 x 9, 368 pp, HC, 978-1-58023-271-5 **$24.99**

Jewish Holidays: A Brief Introduction for Christians
By Rabbi Kerry M. Olitzky and Rabbi Daniel Judson
5½ x 8½, 144 pp, Quality PB, 978-1-58023-302-6 **$16.99**

Reclaiming Judaism as a Spiritual Practice: Holy Days and Shabbat
By Rabbi Goldie Milgram
7 x 9, 272 pp, Quality PB, 978-1-58023-205-0 **$19.99**

7th Heaven: Celebrating Shabbat with Rebbe Nachman of Breslov
By Moshe Mykoff with the Breslov Research Institute
5⅛ x 8¼, 224 pp, Deluxe PB w/flaps, 978-1-58023-175-6 **$18.95**

Shabbat, 2nd Edition: The Family Guide to Preparing for and Celebrating the Sabbath
By Dr. Ron Wolfson 7 x 9, 320 pp, illus., Quality PB, 978-1-58023-164-0 **$19.99**

Hanukkah, 2nd Edition: The Family Guide to Spiritual Celebration
By Dr. Ron Wolfson. Edited by Joel Lurie Grishaver.
7 x 9, 240 pp, illus., Quality PB, 978-1-58023-122-0 **$18.95**

The Jewish Family Fun Book, 2nd Edition: Holiday Projects, Everyday Activities, and Travel Ideas with Jewish Themes *By Danielle Dardashti and Roni Sarig. Illus. by Avi Katz.*
6 x 9, 304 pp, 70+ b/w illus. & diagrams, Quality PB, 978-1-58023-333-0 **$18.99**

The Jewish Lights Book of Fun Classroom Activities: Simple and Seasonal Projects for Teachers and Students *By Danielle Dardashti and Roni Sarig*
6 x 9, 240 pp, Quality PB, 978-1-58023-206-7 **$19.99**

Passover

My People's Passover Haggadah
Traditional Texts, Modern Commentaries
Edited by Rabbi Lawrence A. Hoffman, PhD, and David Arnow, PhD
A diverse and exciting collection of commentaries on the traditional Passover Haggadah—in two volumes!
Vol. 1: 7 x 10, 304 pp, HC, 978-1-58023-354-5 **$24.99**
Vol. 2: 7 x 10, 320 pp, HC, 978-1-58023-346-0 **$24.99**

Leading the Passover Journey
The Seder's Meaning Revealed, the Haggadah's Story Retold
By Rabbi Nathan Laufer
Uncovers the hidden meaning of the Seder's rituals and customs.
6 x 9, 224 pp, HC, 978-1-58023-211-1 **$24.99**

The Women's Passover Companion: Women's Reflections on the Festival of Freedom
Edited by Rabbi Sharon Cohen Anisfeld, Tara Mohr, and Catherine Spector
6 x 9, 352 pp, Quality PB, 978-1-58023-231-9 **$19.99**

The Women's Seder Sourcebook: Rituals & Readings for Use at the Passover Seder
Edited by Rabbi Sharon Cohen Anisfeld, Tara Mohr, and Catherine Spector
6 x 9, 384 pp, Quality PB, 978-1-58023-232-6 **$19.99**

Creating Lively Passover Seders: A Sourcebook of Engaging Tales, Texts & Activities
By David Arnow, PhD 7 x 9, 416 pp, Quality PB, 978-1-58023-184-8 **$24.99**

Passover, 2nd Edition: The Family Guide to Spiritual Celebration
By Dr. Ron Wolfson with Joel Lurie Grishaver 7 x 9, 352 pp, Quality PB, 978-1-58023-174-9 **$19.95**

Life Cycle
Marriage / Parenting / Family / Aging

The New Jewish Baby Album: Creating and Celebrating the Beginning of a Spiritual Life—A Jewish Lights Companion
By the Editors at Jewish Lights. Foreword by Anita Diamant. Preface by Rabbi Sandy Eisenberg Sasso.
A spiritual keepsake that will be treasured for generations. More than just a memory book, *shows you how—and why it's important*—to create a Jewish home and a Jewish life. 8 x 10, 64 pp, Deluxe Padded HC, Full-color illus., 978-1-58023-138-1 **$19.95**

The Jewish Pregnancy Book: A Resource for the Soul, Body & Mind during Pregnancy, Birth & the First Three Months
By Sandy Falk, MD, and Rabbi Daniel Judson, with Steven A. Rapp
Includes medical information, prayers and rituals for each stage of pregnancy, from a liberal Jewish perspective. 7 x 10, 208 pp, Quality PB, b/w photos, 978-1-58023-178-7 **$16.95**

Celebrating Your New Jewish Daughter: Creating Jewish Ways to Welcome Baby Girls into the Covenant—New and Traditional Ceremonies *By Debra Nussbaum Cohen; Foreword by Rabbi Sandy Eisenberg Sasso* 6 x 9, 272 pp, Quality PB, 978-1-58023-090-2 **$18.95**

The New Jewish Baby Book, 2nd Edition: Names, Ceremonies & Customs—A Guide for Today's Families *By Anita Diamant* 6 x 9, 336 pp, Quality PB, 978-1-58023-251-7 **$19.99**

Parenting as a Spiritual Journey: Deepening Ordinary and Extraordinary Events into Sacred Occasions *By Rabbi Nancy Fuchs-Kreimer*
6 x 9, 224 pp, Quality PB, 978-1-58023-016-2 **$16.95**

Parenting Jewish Teens: A Guide for the Perplexed
By Joanne Doades
Explores the questions and issues that shape the world in which today's Jewish teenagers live.
6 x 9, 200 pp, Quality PB, 978-1-58023-305-7 **$16.99**

Judaism for Two: A Spiritual Guide for Strengthening and Celebrating Your Loving Relationship *By Rabbi Nancy Fuchs-Kreimer and Rabbi Nancy H. Wiener; Foreword by Rabbi Elliot N. Dorff* Addresses the ways Jewish teachings can enhance and strengthen committed relationships. 6 x 9, 224 pp, Quality PB, 978-1-58023-254-8 **$16.99**

Embracing the Covenant: Converts to Judaism Talk About Why & How
By Rabbi Allan Berkowitz and Patti Moskovitz 6 x 9, 192 pp, Quality PB, 978-1-879045-50-7 **$16.95**

The Guide to Jewish Interfaith Family Life: An InterfaithFamily.com Handbook
Edited by Ronnie Friedland and Edmund Case 6 x 9, 384 pp, Quality PB, 978-1-58023-153-4 **$18.95**

Introducing My Faith and My Community
The Jewish Outreach Institute Guide for the Christian in a Jewish Interfaith Relationship
By Rabbi Kerry M. Olitzky 6 x 9, 176 pp, Quality PB, 978-1-58023-192-3 **$16.99**

Making a Successful Jewish Interfaith Marriage: The Jewish Outreach Institute Guide to Opportunities, Challenges and Resources *By Rabbi Kerry M. Olitzky with Joan Peterson Littman*
6 x 9, 176 pp, Quality PB, 978-1-58023-170-1 **$16.95**

The Creative Jewish Wedding Book: A Hands-On Guide to New & Old Traditions, Ceremonies & Celebrations *By Gabrielle Kaplan-Mayer*
9 x 9, 288 pp, b/w photos, Quality PB, 978-1-58023-194-7 **$19.99**

Divorce Is a Mitzvah: A Practical Guide to Finding Wholeness and Holiness When Your Marriage Dies *By Rabbi Perry Netter; Afterword by Rabbi Laura Geller.*
6 x 9, 224 pp, Quality PB, 978-1-58023-172-5 **$16.95**

A Heart of Wisdom: Making the Jewish Journey from Midlife through the Elder Years
Edited by Susan Berrin; Foreword by Harold Kushner
6 x 9, 384 pp, Quality PB, 978-1-58023-051-3 **$18.95**

So That Your Values Live On: Ethical Wills and How to Prepare Them
Edited by Jack Riemer and Nathaniel Stampfer
6 x 9, 272 pp, Quality PB, 978-1-879045-34-7 **$18.99**

Spirituality

Journeys to a Jewish Life: Inspiring Stories from the Spiritual Journeys of American Jews *By Paula Amann*
Examines the soul treks of Jews lost and found. 6 x 9, 208 pp, HC, 978-1-58023-317-0 **$19.99**

The Adventures of Rabbi Harvey: A Graphic Novel of Jewish Wisdom and Wit in the Wild West *By Steve Sheinkin*
Jewish and American folktales combine in this witty and original graphic novel collection. Creatively retold and set on the western frontier of the 1870s.
6 x 9, 144 pp, Full-color illus., Quality PB, 978-1-58023-310-1 **$16.99**
Also Available: **The Adventures of Rabbi Harvey Teacher's Guide**
8½ x 11, 32 pp, PB, 978-1-58023-326-2 **$8.99**

Ethics of the Sages: Pirke Avot—Annotated & Explained
Translation and Annotation by Rabbi Rami Shapiro
5½ x 8½, 192 pp, Quality PB, 978-1-59473-207-2 **$16.99** *(A SkyLight Paths book)*

A Book of Life: Embracing Judaism as a Spiritual Practice
By Michael Strassfeld 6 x 9, 528 pp, Quality PB, 978-1-58023-247-0 **$19.99**

Meaning and Mitzvah: Daily Practices for Reclaiming Judaism through Prayer, God, Torah, Hebrew, Mitzvot and Peoplehood *By Rabbi Goldie Milgram*
7 x 9, 336 pp, Quality PB, 978-1-58023-256-2 **$19.99**

The Soul of the Story: Meetings with Remarkable People
By Rabbi David Zeller 6 x 9, 288 pp, HC, 978-1-58023-272-2 **$21.99**

Aleph-Bet Yoga: Embodying the Hebrew Letters for Physical and Spiritual Well-Being
By Steven A. Rapp. Foreword by Tamar Frankiel, PhD and Judy Greenfeld. Preface by Hart Lazer.
7 x 10, 128 pp, b/w photos, Quality PB, Layflat binding, 978-1-58023-162-6 **$16.95**

Does the Soul Survive? A Jewish Journey to Belief in Afterlife, Past Lives & Living with Purpose *By Rabbi Elie Kaplan Spitz; Foreword by Brian L. Weiss, MD*
6 x 9, 288 pp, Quality PB, 978-1-58023-165-7 **$16.99**

First Steps to a New Jewish Spirit: Reb Zalman's Guide to Recapturing the Intimacy & Ecstasy in Your Relationship with God *By Rabbi Zalman M. Schachter-Shalomi with Donald Gropman* 6 x 9, 144 pp, Quality PB, 978-1-58023-182-4 **$16.95**

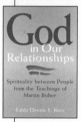

God in Our Relationships: Spirituality between People from the Teachings of Martin Buber *By Rabbi Dennis S. Ross* 5½ x 8½, 160 pp, Quality PB, 978-1-58023-147-3 **$16.95**

Judaism, Physics and God: Searching for Sacred Metaphors in a Post-Einstein World
By Rabbi David W. Nelson 6 x 9, 368 pp, Quality PB, inc. reader's discussion guide, 978-1-58023-306-4 **$18.99**;
HC, 352 pp, 978-1-58023-252-4 **$24.99**

The Jewish Lights Spirituality Handbook: A Guide to Understanding, Exploring & Living a Spiritual Life *Edited by Stuart M. Matlins*
What exactly is "Jewish" about spirituality? How do I make it a part of my life? Fifty of today's foremost spiritual leaders share their ideas and experience with us.
6 x 9, 456 pp, Quality PB, 978-1-58023-093-3 **$19.99**

Bringing the Psalms to Life: How to Understand and Use the Book of Psalms
By Daniel F. Polish 6 x 9, 208 pp, Quality PB, 978-1-58023-157-2 **$16.95**;
HC, 978-1-58023-077-3 **$21.95**

God & the Big Bang: Discovering Harmony between Science & Spirituality
By Daniel C. Matt 6 x 9, 216 pp, Quality PB, 978-1-879045-89-7 **$16.99**

Minding the Temple of the Soul: Balancing Body, Mind, and Spirit through Traditional Jewish Prayer, Movement, and Meditation *By Tamar Frankiel, PhD, and Judy Greenfeld*
7 x 10, 184 pp, illus., Quality PB, 978-1-879045-64-4 **$16.95**
Audiotape of the Blessings and Meditations: 60 min. **$9.95**
Videotape of the Movements and Meditations: 46 min. **$20.00**

One God Clapping: The Spiritual Path of a Zen Rabbi *By Alan Lew with Sherril Jaffe*
5½ x 8½, 336 pp, Quality PB, 978-1-58023-115-2 **$16.95**

There Is No Messiah ... and You're It: The Stunning Transformation of Judaism's Most Provocative Idea *By Rabbi Robert N. Levine, DD*
6 x 9, 192 pp, Quality PB, 978-1-58023-255-5 **$16.99**

These Are the Words: A Vocabulary of Jewish Spiritual Life
By Arthur Green 6 x 9, 304 pp, Quality PB, 978-1-58023-107-7 **$18.95**

Spirituality/Women's Interest

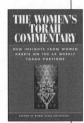

The Quotable Jewish Woman: Wisdom, Inspiration & Humor from the Mind & Heart
Edited and compiled by Elaine Bernstein Partnow
6 x 9, 496 pp, Quality PB, 978-1-58023-236-4 **$19.99**; HC, 978-1-58023-193-0 **$29.99**

The Divine Feminine in Biblical Wisdom Literature: Selections Annotated & Explained *Translated and Annotated by Rabbi Rami Shapiro*
5½ x 8½, 240 pp, Quality PB, 978-1-59473-109-9 **$16.99** (A SkyLight Paths book)

The Women's Haftarah Commentary: New Insights from Women Rabbis on the 54 Weekly Haftarah Portions, the 5 Megillot & Special Shabbatot
Edited by Rabbi Elyse Goldstein 6 x 9, 560 pp, HC, 978-1-58023-133-6 **$39.99**

The Women's Torah Commentary: New Insights from Women Rabbis on the 54 Weekly Torah Portions *Edited by Rabbi Elyse Goldstein*
6 x 9, 496 pp, HC, 978-1-58023-076-6 **$34.95**

The Year Mom Got Religion: One Woman's Midlife Journey into Judaism
By Lee Meyerhoff Hendler 6 x 9, 208 pp, Quality PB, 978-1-58023-070-4 **$15.95**

See Holidays for *The Women's Passover Companion: Women's Reflections on the Festival of Freedom* and *The Women's Seder Sourcebook: Rituals & Readings for Use at the Passover Seder.* Also see Bar/Bat Mitzvah for *The JGirl's Guide: The Young Jewish Woman's Handbook for Coming of Age.*

Spirituality / Crafts

(from SkyLight Paths, our sister imprint)

The Knitting Way: A Guide to Spiritual Self-Discovery
By Linda Skolnick and Janice MacDaniels
Shows how to use the practice of knitting to strengthen our spiritual selves.
7 x 9, 240 pp, Quality PB, 978-1-59473-079-5 **$16.99**

The Quilting Path: A Guide to Spiritual Self-Discovery through Fabric, Thread and Kabbalah *By Louise Silk*
Explores how to cultivate personal growth through quilt making.
7 x 9, 192 pp, Quality PB, 978-1-59473-206-5 **$16.99**

The Painting Path: Embodying Spiritual Discovery through Yoga, Brush and Color *By Linda Novick; Foreword by Richard Segalman*
Explores the divine connection you can experience through art.
7 x 9, 208 pp, 8-page full-color insert, Quality PB, 978-1-59473-226-3 **$18.99**

The Scrapbooking Journey: A Hands-On Guide to Spiritual Discovery
By Cory Richardson-Lauve; Foreword by Stacy Julian
Reveals how this craft can become a practice used to deepen and shape your life.
7 x 9, 176 pp, 8-page full-color insert, b/w photos, Quality PB, 978-1-59473-216-4 **$18.99**

Travel

Israel—A Spiritual Travel Guide, 2nd Edition
A Companion for the Modern Jewish Pilgrim
By Rabbi Lawrence A. Hoffman 4¾ x 10, 256 pp, Quality PB, illus., 978-1-58023-261-6 **$18.99**
Also Available: **The Israel Mission Leader's Guide** 978-1-58023-085-8 **$4.95**

12-Step

100 Blessings Every Day: Daily Twelve Step Recovery Affirmations, Exercises for Personal Growth & Renewal Reflecting Seasons of the Jewish Year
By Rabbi Kerry M. Olitzky; Foreword by Rabbi Neil Gillman
4½ x 6½, 432 pp, Quality PB, 978-1-879045-30-9 **$16.99**

Recovery from Codependence: A Jewish Twelve Steps Guide to Healing Your Soul
By Rabbi Kerry M. Olitzky 6 x 9, 160 pp, Quality PB, 978-1-879045-32-3 **$13.95**

Twelve Jewish Steps to Recovery: A Personal Guide to Turning from Alcoholism & Other Addictions—Drugs, Food, Gambling, Sex ...
By Rabbi Kerry M. Olitzky and Stuart A. Copans, MD; Preface by Abraham J. Twerski, MD
6 x 9, 144 pp, Quality PB, 978-1-879045-09-5 **$15.99**

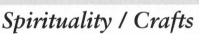

Spirituality/Lawrence Kushner

Filling Words with Light: Hasidic and Mystical Reflections on Jewish Prayer
By Lawrence Kushner and Nehemia Polen
5½ x 8½, 176 pp, Quality PB, 978-1-58023-238-8 **$16.99**; HC, 978-1-58023-216-6 **$21.99**

The Book of Letters: A Mystical Hebrew Alphabet
Popular HC Edition, 6 x 9, 80 pp, 2-color text, 978-1-879045-00-2 **$24.95**
Collector's Limited Edition, 9 x 12, 80 pp, gold foil embossed pages, w/limited edition silkscreened print, 978-1-879045-04-0 **$349.00**

The Book of Miracles: A Young Person's Guide to Jewish Spiritual Awareness
6 x 9, 96 pp, 2-color illus., HC, 978-1-879045-78-1 **$16.95** *For ages 9 and up*

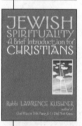

The Book of Words: Talking Spiritual Life, Living Spiritual Talk
6 x 9, 160 pp, Quality PB, 978-1-58023-020-9 **$16.95**

Eyes Remade for Wonder: A Lawrence Kushner Reader *Introduction by Thomas Moore*
6 x 9, 240 pp, Quality PB, 978-1-58023-042-1 **$18.95**

God Was in This Place & I, i Did Not Know: Finding Self, Spirituality and Ultimate Meaning 6 x 9, 192 pp, Quality PB, 978-1-879045-33-0 **$16.95**

Honey from the Rock: An Introduction to Jewish Mysticism
6 x 9, 176 pp, Quality PB, 978-1-58023-073-5 **$16.95**

Invisible Lines of Connection: Sacred Stories of the Ordinary
5½ x 8½, 160 pp, Quality PB, 978-1-879045-98-9 **$15.95**

Jewish Spirituality—A Brief Introduction for Christians
5½ x 8½, 112 pp, Quality PB, 978-1-58023-150-3 **$12.95**

The River of Light: Jewish Mystical Awareness
6 x 9, 192 pp, Quality PB, 978-1-58023-096-4 **$16.95**

The Way Into Jewish Mystical Tradition
6 x 9, 224 pp, Quality PB, 978-1-58023-200-5 **$18.99**; HC, 978-1-58023-029-2 **$21.95**

Spirituality/Prayer

My People's Passover Haggadah: Traditional Texts, Modern Commentaries
Edited by Rabbi Lawrence A. Hoffman, PhD, and David Arnow, PhD Diverse commentaries
on the traditional Passover Haggadah—in two volumes! Vol. 1: 7 x 10, 304 pp, HC
978-1-58023-354-5 **$24.99** Vol. 2: 7 x 10, 320 pp, HC, 978-1-58023-346-0 **$24.99**

Witnesses to the One: The Spiritual History of the *Sh'ma* *By Rabbi Joseph B. Meszler; Foreword by Rabbi Elyse Goldstein* 6 x 9, 176 pp, HC, 978-1-58023-309-5 **$19.99**

My People's Prayer Book Series

Traditional Prayers, Modern Commentaries *Edited by Rabbi Lawrence A. Hoffman*
Provides diverse and exciting commentary to the traditional liturgy, helping modern
men and women find new wisdom in Jewish prayer, and bring liturgy into their lives.
Each book includes Hebrew text, modern translation, and commentaries from all
perspectives of the Jewish world.

Vol. 1—The *Sh'ma* and Its Blessings
7 x 10, 168 pp, HC, 978-1-879045-79-8 **$24.99**
Vol. 2—The *Amidah*
7 x 10, 240 pp, HC, 978-1-879045-80-4 **$24.95**
Vol. 3—*P'sukei D'zimrah* (Morning Psalms)
7 x 10, 240 pp, HC, 978-1-879045-81-1 **$24.95**
Vol. 4—*Seder K'riat Hatorah* (The Torah Service)
7 x 10, 264 pp, HC, 978-1-879045-82-8 **$23.95**
Vol. 5—*Birkhot Hashachar* (Morning Blessings)
7 x 10, 240 pp, HC, 978-1-879045-83-5 **$24.95**
Vol. 6—*Tachanun* and Concluding Prayers
7 x 10, 240 pp, HC, 978-1-879045-84-2 **$24.95**
Vol. 7—Shabbat at Home
7 x 10, 240 pp, HC, 978-1-879045-85-9 **$24.95**
Vol. 8—*Kabbalat Shabbat* (Welcoming Shabbat in the Synagogue)
7 x 10, 240 pp, HC, 978-1-58023-121-3 **$24.99**
Vol. 9—Welcoming the Night: *Minchah* and *Ma'ariv* (Afternoon and
Evening Prayer) 7 x 10, 272 pp, HC, 978-1-58023-262-3 **$24.99**
Vol. 10—Shabbat Morning: *Shacharit* and *Musaf* (Morning and
Additional Services) 7 x 10, 240 pp, HC, 978-1-58023-240-1 **$24.99**

Judaism / Christianity / Interfaith

Talking about God: Exploring the Meaning of Religious Life with Kierkegaard, Buber, Tillich and Heschel *by Daniel F. Polish, PhD*
Examines the meaning of the human religious experience with the greatest theologians of modern times. 6 x 9, 176 pp, HC, 978-1-59473-230-0 **$21.99** (a SkyLight Paths book)

Interactive Faith: The Essential Interreligious Community-Building Handbook
Edited by Rev. Bud Heckman with Rori Picker Neiss
A guide to the key methods and resources of the interfaith movement.
6 x 9, 400 pp (est), HC, 978-1-59473-237-9 **$40.00** (a SkyLight Paths book)

The Jewish Approach to Repairing the World (*Tikkun Olam*)
A Brief Introduction for Christians *by Rabbi Elliot N. Dorff, PhD*
A window into the Jewish idea of responsibility to care for the world.
5½ x 8½, 192 pp (est), Quality PB, 978-1-58023-349-1 **$16.99**

Modern Jews Engage the New Testament: Enhancing Jewish Well-Being in a Christian Environment *by Rabbi Michael J. Cook, PhD*
A look at the dynamics of the New Testament.
6 x 9, 416 pp, HC, 978-1-58023-313-2 **$29.99**

Disaster Spiritual Care: Practical Clergy Responses to Community, Regional and National Tragedy
Edited by Rabbi Stephen B. Roberts, BCJC, & Rev. Willard W.C. Ashley, Sr., DMin, DH
The definitive reference for pastoral caregivers of all faiths involved in disaster response.
6 x 9, 384 pp, Hardcover, 978-1-59473-240-9 **$40.00** (a SkyLight Paths book)

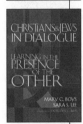

The Changing Christian World: A Brief Introduction for Jews
by Rabbi Leonard A. Schoolman
5½ x 8½, 176 pp, Quality PB, 978-1-58023-344-6 **$16.99**

The Jewish Connection to Israel, the Promised Land: A Brief Introduction for Christians *by Rabbi Eugene Korn, PhD*
5½ x 8½, 192 pp, Quality PB, 978-1-58023-318-7 **$14.99**

Christians and Jews in Dialogue: Learning in the Presence of the Other
by Mary C. Boys and Sara S. Lee; Foreword by Dorothy C. Bass
Inspires renewed commitment to dialogue between religious traditions.
6 x 9, 240 pp, HC, 978-1-59473-144-0 **$21.99** (a SkyLight Paths book)

Healing the Jewish-Christian Rift: Growing Beyond Our Wounded History
by Ron Miller and Laura Bernstein; Foreword by Dr. Beatrice Bruteau
6 x 9, 288 pp, Quality PB, 978-1-59473-139-6 **$18.99** (a SkyLight Paths book)

Introducing My Faith and My Community
The Jewish Outreach Institute Guide for the Christian in a Jewish Interfaith Relationship
by Rabbi Kerry M. Olitzky 6 x 9, 176 pp, Quality PB, 978-1-58023-192-3 **$16.99**

The Jewish Approach to God: A Brief Introduction for Christians
by Rabbi Neil Gillman 5½ x 8½, 192 pp, Quality PB, 978-1-58023-190-9 **$16.95**

Jewish Holidays: A Brief Introduction for Christians
by Rabbi Kerry M. Olitzky and Rabbi Daniel Judson
5½ x 8½, 176 pp, Quality PB, 978-1-58023-302-6 **$16.99**

Jewish Ritual: A Brief Introduction for Christians
by Rabbi Kerry M. Olitzky and Rabbi Daniel Judson
5½ x 8½, 144 pp, Quality PB, 978-1-58023-210-4 **$14.99**

Jewish Spirituality: A Brief Introduction for Christians *by Rabbi Lawrence Kushner*
5½ x 8½, 112 pp, Quality PB, 978-1-58023-150-3 **$12.95**

A Jewish Understanding of the New Testament
by Rabbi Samuel Sandmel; new Preface by Rabbi David Sandmel
5½ x 8½, 368 pp, Quality PB, 978-1-59473-048-1 **$19.99** (a SkyLight Paths book)

We Jews and Jesus: Exploring Theological Differences for Mutual Understanding
by Rabbi Samuel Sandmel; new Preface by Rabbi David Sandmel A Classic Reprint
6 x 9, 192 pp, Quality PB, 978-1-59473-208-9 **$16.99** (a SkyLight Paths book)

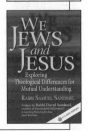

Show Me Your Way: The Complete Guide to Exploring Interfaith Spiritual Direction
by Howard A. Addison 5½ x 8½, 240 pp, Quality PB, 978-1-893361-41-6 **$16.95** (a SkyLight Paths book)

Theology/Philosophy/The Way Into... Series

The Way Into... series offers an accessible and highly usable "guided tour" of the Jewish faith, people, history and beliefs—in total, an introduction to Judaism that will enable you to understand and interact with the sacred texts of the Jewish tradition. Each volume is written by a leading contemporary scholar and teacher, and explores one key aspect of Judaism. The Way Into... series enables all readers to achieve a real sense of Jewish cultural literacy through guided study.

The Way Into Encountering God in Judaism
By Neil Gillman
For everyone who wants to understand how Jews have encountered God throughout history and today.
6 x 9, 240 pp, Quality PB, 978-1-58023-199-2 **$18.99**; HC, 978-1-58023-025-4 **$21.95**
Also Available: **The Jewish Approach to God:** A Brief Introduction for Christians
By Neil Gillman
5½ x 8½, 192 pp, Quality PB, 978-1-58023-190-9 **$16.95**

The Way Into Jewish Mystical Tradition
By Lawrence Kushner
Allows readers to interact directly with the sacred mystical text of the Jewish tradition. An accessible introduction to the concepts of Jewish mysticism, their religious and spiritual significance and how they relate to life today.
6 x 9, 224 pp, Quality PB, 978-1-58023-200-5 **$18.99**; HC, 978-1-58023-029-2 **$21.95**

The Way Into Jewish Prayer
By Lawrence A. Hoffman
Opens the door to 3,000 years of Jewish prayer, making available all anyone needs to feel at home in the Jewish way of communicating with God.
6 x 9, 208 pp, Quality PB, 978-1-58023-201-2 **$18.99**
Also Available: **The Way Into Jewish Prayer Teacher's Guide**
By Rabbi Jennifer Ossakow Goldsmith
8½ x 11, 42 pp, PB, 978-1-58023-345-3 **$8.99**
Visit our website to download a free copy.

The Way Into Judaism and the Environment
By Jeremy Benstein
Explores the ways in which Judaism contributes to contemporary social-environmental issues, the extent to which Judaism is part of the problem and how it can be part of the solution.
6 x 9, 288 pp, HC, 978-1-58023-268-5 **$24.99**

The Way Into Tikkun Olam (Repairing the World)
By Elliot N. Dorff
An accessible introduction to the Jewish concept of the individual's responsibility to care for others and repair the world.
6 x 9, 320 pp, HC, 978-1-58023-269-2 **$24.99**; 304 pp, Quality PB, 978-1-58023-328-6 **$18.99**

The Way Into Torah
By Norman J. Cohen
Helps guide in the exploration of the origins and development of Torah, explains why it should be studied and how to do it.
6 x 9, 176 pp, Quality PB, 978-1-58023-198-5 **$16.99**

The Way Into the Varieties of Jewishness
By Sylvia Barack Fishman, PhD
Explores the religious and historical understanding of what it has meant to be Jewish from ancient times to the present controversy over "Who is a Jew?"
6 x 9, 288 pp, HC, 978-1-58023-030-8 **$24.99**

Theology/Philosophy

A Touch of the Sacred: A Theologian's Informal Guide to Jewish Belief
By Dr. Eugene B. Borowitz and Frances W. Schwartz Explores the musings from the
leading theologian of liberal Judaism. 6 x 9, 256 pp, HC, 978-1-58023-337-8 **$21.99**

Talking about God: Exploring the Meaning of Religious Life with
Kierkegaard, Buber, Tillich and Heschel *By Daniel F. Polish, PhD*
Examines the meaning of the human religious experience with the greatest theologians of modern times. 6 x 9, 160 pp, HC, 978-1-59473-230-0 **$21.99** *(A SkyLight Paths book)*

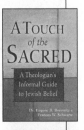

Jews & Judaism in the 21st Century: Human Responsibility, the
Presence of God, and the Future of the Covenant
Edited by Rabbi Edward Feinstein; Foreword by Paula E. Hyman
Five celebrated leaders in Judaism examine contemporary Jewish life.
6 x 9, 192 pp, HC, 978-1-58023-315-6 **$24.99**

Christians and Jews in Dialogue: Learning in the Presence of the Other
By Mary C. Boys and Sara S. Lee; Foreword by Dr. Dorothy Bass
6 x 9, 240 pp, HC, 978-1-59473-144-0 **$21.99** *(A SkyLight Paths book)*

The Death of Death: Resurrection and Immortality in Jewish Thought
By Neil Gillman 6 x 9, 336 pp, Quality PB, 978-1-58023-081-0 **$18.95**

Ethics of the Sages: Pirke Avot—Annotated & Explained
Translation & Annotation by Rabbi Rami Shapiro
5½ x 8½, 208 pp, Quality PB, 978-1-59473-207-2 **$16.99** *(A SkyLight Paths book)*

Hasidic Tales: Annotated & Explained
By Rabbi Rami Shapiro; Foreword by Andrew Harvey
5½ x 8½, 240 pp, Quality PB, 978-1-893361-86-7 **$16.95** *(A SkyLight Paths Book)*

A Heart of Many Rooms: Celebrating the Many Voices within Judaism
By David Hartman 6 x 9, 352 pp, Quality PB, 978-1-58023-156-5 **$19.95**

The Hebrew Prophets: Selections Annotated & Explained
Translation & Annotation by Rabbi Rami Shapiro; Foreword by Zalman M. Schachter-Shalomi
5½ x 8½, 224 pp, Quality PB, 978-1-59473-037-5 **$16.99** *(A SkyLight Paths book)*

A Jewish Understanding of the New Testament
By Rabbi Samuel Sandmel; Preface by David Sandmel
5½ x 8½, 368 pp, Quality PB, 978-1-59473-048-1 **$19.99** *(A SkyLight Paths book)*

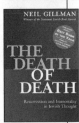

Keeping Faith with the Psalms: Deepen Your Relationship with God Using the Book
of Psalms *By Daniel F. Polish* 6 x 9, 320 pp, Quality PB, 978-1-58023-300-2 **$18.99**

A Living Covenant: The Innovative Spirit in Traditional Judaism
By David Hartman 6 x 9, 368 pp, Quality PB, 978-1-58023-011-7 **$20.00**

Love and Terror in the God Encounter
The Theological Legacy of Rabbi Joseph B. Soloveitchik
By David Hartman 6 x 9, 240 pp, Quality PB, 978-1-58023-176-3 **$19.95**

The Personhood of God: Biblical Theology, Human Faith and the Divine Image
By Dr. Yochanan Muffs; Foreword by Dr. David Hartman 6 x 9, 240 pp, HC, 978-1-58023-265-4 **$24.99**

Traces of God: Seeing God in Torah, History and Everyday Life
By Neil Gillman 6 x 9, 240 pp, HC, 978-1-58023-249-4 **$21.99**

We Jews and Jesus: Exploring Theological Differences for Mutual Understanding
By Rabbi Samuel Sandmel; Preface by Rabbi David Sandmel
6 x 9, 176 pp, Quality PB, 978-1-59473-208-9 **$16.99** *(A SkyLight Paths book)*

Your Word Is Fire: The Hasidic Masters on Contemplative Prayer
Edited and translated by Arthur Green and Barry W. Holtz
6 x 9, 160 pp, Quality PB, 978-1-879045-25-5 **$15.95**

I Am Jewish
Personal Reflections Inspired by the Last Words of Daniel Pearl
Almost 150 Jews—both famous and not—from all walks of life, from all around
the world, write about many aspects of their Judaism.
Edited by Judea and Ruth Pearl
6 x 9, 304 pp, Deluxe PB w/flaps, 978-1-58023-259-3 **$18.99**
Download a free copy of the *I Am Jewish Teacher's Guide* at our website:
www.jewishlights.com

JEWISH LIGHTS BOOKS ARE AVAILABLE FROM BETTER BOOKSTORES. TRY YOUR BOOKSTORE FIRST.

About Jewish Lights

People of all faiths and backgrounds yearn for books that attract, engage, educate, and spiritually inspire.

Our principal goal is to stimulate thought and help all people learn about who the Jewish People are, where they come from, and what the future can be made to hold. While people of our diverse Jewish heritage are the primary audience, our books speak to people in the Christian world as well and will broaden their understanding of Judaism and the roots of their own faith.

We bring to you authors who are at the forefront of spiritual thought and experience. While each has something different to say, they all say it in a voice that you can hear.

Our books are designed to welcome you and then to engage, stimulate, and inspire. We judge our success not only by whether or not our books are beautiful and commercially successful, but by whether or not they make a difference in your life.

For your information and convenience, at the back of this book we have provided a list of other Jewish Lights books you might find interesting and useful. They cover all the categories of your life:

Bar/Bat Mitzvah
Bible Study / Midrash
Children's Books
Congregation Resources
Current Events / History
Ecology/ Environment
Fiction: Mystery, Science Fiction
Grief / Healing
Holidays / Holy Days
Inspiration
Kabbalah / Mysticism / Enneagram

Life Cycle
Meditation
Parenting
Prayer
Ritual / Sacred Practice
Spirituality
Theology / Philosophy
Travel
12-Step
Women's Interest

Stuart M. Matlins

Stuart M. Matlins, Publisher

Or phone, fax, mail or e-mail to: **JEWISH LIGHTS Publishing**
Sunset Farm Offices, Route 4 • P.O. Box 237 • Woodstock, Vermont 05091
Tel: (802) 457-4000 • Fax: (802) 457-4004 • www.jewishlights.com
Credit card orders: (800) 962-4544 (8:30AM–5:30PM ET Monday–Friday)
Generous discounts on quantity orders. SATISFACTION GUARANTEED. Prices subject to change.

For more information about each book, visit our website at www.jewishlights.com